Canvas Labyrinths

Construction Manual

Robert Ferré

© Contents protected by copyright
Digital Veriditas Edition: 2014

Robert D. Ferre

ISBN (print version)
978-1-940875-99-6

All rights reserved. No part of this publication may be reproduced or transmitted in any form, except for short excerpts used in reviews, without written permission from the publisher.

Published by Labyrinth Enterprises, LLC

www.labyrinth-enterprises.com
San Antonio, Texas

New Veriditas Digital Edition

I made my first canvas labyrinth in 1995 at the urging of the Rev. Dr. Lauren Artress, who had just founded Veriditas, a nonprofit organization to train facilitators and promote the effective use of labyrinths. That request led to my becoming a full time labyrinth maker, with Veriditas as my first client.

Both Veriditas and my company, Labyrinth Enterprises, LLC (originally the St. Louis Labyrinth Project), have been through many changes over the years. We've had good times and lean times. We've traveled together in France and Germany, visiting Chartres Cathedral and Hildegard of Bingen sites. Through it all, my assistants and I supplied Veriditas with canvas labyrinths, hundreds of them.

Lauren and Robert: A light moment together at Maison St. Yves. in Chartres.

Now, I'm mostly retired, and Lauren is heading in the same direction. Capable hands have honed Veriditas into an effective organization with deeply meaningful events. A number of master teachers are adding to the thousands of facilitators already trained.

I'm passing my duties as a labyrinth maker to colleagues whom I've helped train and who will likewise continue carrying the torch for the next generation. Every summer I give a labyrinth making master class for Veriditas (see www.veriditas.org).

I'm contributing all of the proceeds from my labyrinth books, updated and reissued in special digital editions, to Veriditas. I can think of no better tribute to honor the two decades we have worked together.

Robert D. Ferré

The Labyrinth Series

Five books written by Robert D. Ferré, part of the Labyrinth Series published by Labyrinth Enterprises, LLC, are currently being reissued in a digital format for the Veriditas Edition. All should be complete by the end of 2014.

The Labyrinth Revival: A Personal History
    First edition: 1997
    Second edition: 2002
    Digital Veriditas Edition: 2014

Church Labyrinths: Questions & answers regarding the history, relevance, and use of labyrinths in churches
    First edition: 2001
    Digital edition: 2013
    Digital Veriditas Edition: To be released in 2014

Origin, Symbolism, and Design of the Chartres Labyrinth
    First edition: 2001
    Digital Veriditas edition: Planned for 2014

Chartres Labyrinth: Construction Manual
    First edition: 2001
    Revised edition: 2003
    Digital Veriditas edition: Planned for 2014

Classical Labyrinths: Construction Manual
    First edition: 2002
    Digital Veriditas edition: Planned for 2014

Dedication

I dedicate this book to my colleagues in the world of labyrinth building. Their names are sprinkled liberally throughout this book. It's been a pleasure to learn from them, train them, and collaborate on many projects. I appreciate the many suggestions and photographs they contributed to this book.

Second, I dedicate these pages to all my clients, customers, and students who have enabled me to actually make a living as a full time labyrinth maker. They have prodded me, encouraged me, and most of all, paid me for doing work that I love.

Most of all, I dedicate this construction manual to Judy Hopen. It's impossible to think of canvas labyrinths without acknowledging the immense contribution that Judy made to the field. For fifteen years she crawled on hands and knees or bent in half at the waist or pushed herself on a dolly to draw and paint half a million square feet of canvas.

Judy's work and dedication were incomparable. As her legacy, hundreds of thousands of walkers have passed between the lines that she so carefully executed. Thanks, Judy, for all you did for labyrinths and for Labyrinth Enterprises, LLC.

Table of Contents

Introduction	9
Overview	11
Canvas	21
Tools	37
Painting	55
A Tribute to Judy Hopen	67
Gallery	73
Care Instructions	77
Renting Your Labyrinth	83
Addendum	91
Drawing Instructions	95
Business Advice	109
Resources	111
Postscript	113
Photo Credits	114

Greetings reader,

I always like to see authors' workspaces. Here's mine. The bookcase on the left is labyrinth books, and on the right, books about Chartres Cathedral and the Middle Ages. The unseen wall further to the right has a work table, piled high with projects of various sorts. My laser printer is tucked under the folding table that serves as my desk. Through the shutters I've a view of the side of the neighbor's house (brick). Much of my writing happens while I'm traveling, especially on cruise ships. Still, it's always a delight getting back to home base.

This office is the site of much of my writing. Making labyrinths, of course, takes place in many venues. Canvas labyrinths, as described in these pages, are made in large, indoor spaces, such as our first studio, shown left.

Robert D. Ferré

Introduction

Portable labyrinths are a twentieth century American invention. Oh, perhaps someone somewhere made a drawing of a labyrinth on canvas or linen or hemp, but it would just be a fluke. In the United States, it became an industry.

The history of canvas labyrinths isn't really relevant to the topic of this book. For more details, see *The Labyrinth Revival*. When I first started out there were no tools or techniques available, I had to make or adapt them from other purposes. You will see many of them in these pages.

I shouldn't be the one writing this book. It should be Judy Hopen, the world's greatest and most skilled canvas labyrinth drawer and painter. She personally made some eight hundred labyrinths, likely more than anyone in history. Yes, there is a company that prints them that has sold more, but I'm talking works of art, made on hands and knees, hour after day after month for fifteen years.

Sadly, we lost Judy to breast cancer (at the age of fifty-one) in 2012. It was she who ran our studio, the only such studio of its size (8,000 square feet) in existence, dedicated solely to the production of canvas labyrinths. I'm sure there are many little details that Judy would have added to my descriptions. Alas, we have very few photographs of the process. Still, this book should be sufficient for you to make your own canvas labyrinth, whether for personal use or as a business for clients.

Now mostly retired, I no longer have the studio. Others are taking up the call to make what we once made in such profusion. I'm happy to instruct anyone interested in making labyrinths of any kind, and continue to do so in a multi-day master class every summer at Veriditas headquarters in Petaluma, California. Yet, even there, canvas labyrinths are only briefly touched upon. Hence the need for this book.

It began as a few chapters in one of my other labyrinth books, which kept expanding until I realized it should be a separate volume. Some of our work, and photos of our studios, can be seen on our website, www.labyrinth-enterprises.com.

One person I know painted a labyrinth on a tarp freehand, with cans of spray paint. It was horribly misshapen, yet hundreds of people walked it and had meaningful experiences. So don't wait until you feel you are an expert. Go ahead and make a labyrinth, and then another, and another. Let your knowledge and skill develop organically, through trial and error. Hopefully these instructions will limit the range of error and will encourage you.

Having completed this the first edition, I'm especially interested in getting feedback and suggestions. Thanks to the convenience of digital publishing, I can easily make changes to this book and update the information, which I plan to do regularly. Please send me your input about both what works and what doesn't, what's clear and what is confusing, what should be added or subtracted, to:

robert@labyrinth-enterprises.com

Many thanks for your assistance.

Overview

Before you can begin working on your canvas labyrinth, a certain amount of preparation is necessary. All the topics mentioned here will be covered in much greater detail in subsequent chapters. In the above photo I'm giving a workshop in the foreground while Judy Hopen, my assistant and studio manager, is working on a canvas labyrinth in the background. To the rear left is another canvas, covered with plastic to protect it from our occasional roof leaks.

Canvas

I recommend #12 natural untreated cotton duck canvas. It's the same canvas that many artists use (although in this case, without gesso or any other primer). It comes in a number of widths and lengths, which will be determined by the size labyrinth you intend to make.

While a portable labyrinth can be drawn on just about any type of cloth (sheets, tarps, parachutes, drop cloths), duck canvas is by far the most practical, as it has good body, lies flat, and holds paint well.

One drawback can be the weight. Although #12 is the lightest of the numbered ducks (1-12, the lower the number the heavier the material), it still weighs approximately 10.5 to 11.0 ounces per square yard. If you have a 30-foot piece of canvas, that equals almost 70 pounds. The Velcro® and paint add additional weight.

I experimented with many lightweight fabrics to make a compact travel labyrinth, but such fabrics don't lie well, the push and wrinkle when walking them, they require ink rather than paint, and are hard to draw on. Even searching for a vinyl material that would be usable outdoors, weight became too much of an issue.

Canvas is a material that should be used indoors. It's hard to clean, and tends toward mildew when it gets damp. If you are intending to use your labyrinth outdoors, you might consider constructing a temporary one rather than using canvas. (See our manuals on constructing the Chartres and classical labyrinths).

Sewing

At the very least you will want to be hemming the perimeter of the canvas. If you are making a labyrinth over 12' (twelve feet) in diameter, there will be multiple panels that will need to be sewn together or attached in some way.

The amount of sewing required depends on a number of factors, especially the size of the labyrinth and the width of the canvas. If you want a labyrinth that is a single piece, then panels will need to be sewn together. Our sewing contractors in St. Louis had a nifty machine that joined the panels (double row of stitching) with a simple overlap of the two pieces, without any bulky rolling (such as a French Seam).

You can buy canvas as wide as 12'. In such case, a 24' labyrinth would only need one seam. If you are considering a 36' canvas, then you may want to make three pieces that Velcro® together.

You must consider seams, Velcro®, and hems. Who can do this work? It takes special equipment and very large tables to deal with so much fabric. Sail makers and tarp makers would be good prospects. Tent makers, too, or a custom company that is geared for doing large pieces. If in doubt, you can always use the sewing company we used in St. Louis and have them ship the canvas to you with the panels and Velcro® in place (to be hemmed later). They are:
>Mickley's Canvas Products
>9523 Watson Industrial Park
>St. Louis, MO 63126
>(314) 963-0800

Say hello to Bryan and Don from me. They are a father/son team (in business for more than sixty years).

Sewing the canvas takes a big table.

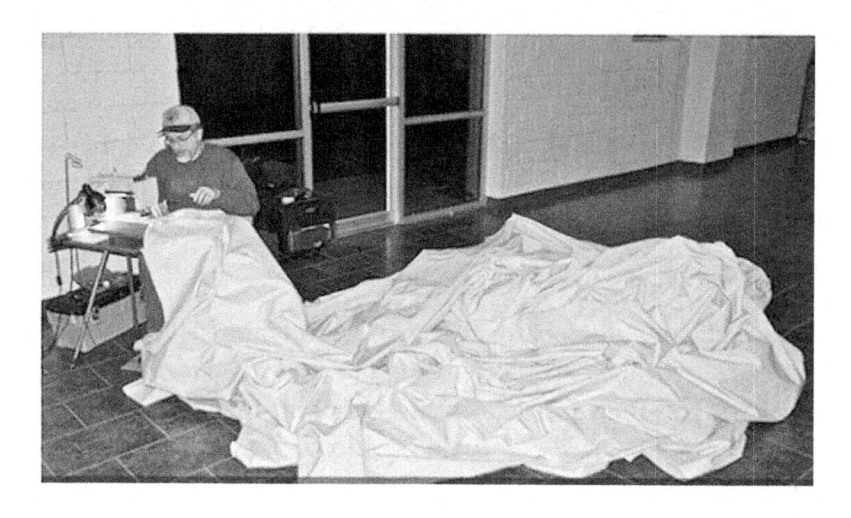

Or maybe it doesn't take a big table, as John Ridder demonstrates.

I know people who have sewn their own canvas. It takes a heavy duty machine. If you buy wide canvas, you can limit the sewing to hemming and Velcro®, both of which are around the perimeter. It's less technical than trying to sew panels together.

Workspace

Canvas labyrinths require larges spaces, for both making and walking. For smaller ones, a living room might be sufficient, or a two-car garage. For larger ones, a basketball court works well. Airplane hangers have lots of space.

If you are only making one labyrinth, or even a few, you can usually find a space to use for a few days. Church meeting halls are good candidates, clean and climatized. One group found space at the local National Guard Armory. I made a canvas labyrinth in Australia outside, on asphalt pavement, which is not ideal but can work in a pinch if the surface is smooth and covered with a clean tarp, and the weather favorable. The kookaburras seemed to enjoy it.

It's possible to draw the labyrinth in a borrowed space, and then paint it in a different, smaller space, by painting one section at a time.

Grade school students in Hawaii painting a canvas labyrinth as directed by Lars Howlett.

Special tools

I'd love to go down to Sears and buy Craftsman labyrinth making tools, but there is no such thing. Some tools are available, such as mechanical pencils and paint brushes, but others need to be constructed, including a compass and long straightedges. I'll go into some detail about tools, as they are very important.

Drawing procedures

Unabated, the canvas will move and slide around the floor when you attempt to draw on it, making your job almost impossible. Likewise, if you try to paint, the canvass will pucker up and shrink.

When artists paint on canvas, they stretch it across a frame or glue it to something rigid. To make a canvas labyrinth, we must also do something to stretch the canvas and hold it in place .

Once the canvas is secured, we aren't quite ready to draw yet. Pencils, even soft ones drawn lightly, are very hard to erase from canvas. So, we need to mark the places on the canvas where we stop the circles for the entrance or the turns, thereby eliminating the need for erasing.

We also will work in our stocking feet (or with disposable paper shoe covers) to help keep the canvas clean. Alternatively, you could have shoes that are worn only on the canvas (could I suggest canvas sneakers?). It's best to avoid walking on the drawn pencil lines, as they will smudge, and cause more erasing.

The drawing itself goes quite quickly. Of course, some patterns are harder than others. The preparation and the painting tend to be more time consuming than the actual drawing. I won't be covering the geometry or highly detailed instructions for drawing labyrinths in these pages. I have other books dedicated to those topics. The purpose of this book is to make clear the process of making canvas labyrinths.

Painting

The answer is: indoor flat latex paint. The question was, what sort of paint do I use? That's my most asked question. (Remember Steve Allen on television making up questions when given the answer? One answer was "UCLA," to which he made up the question, "What do you see when the fog lifts?" But I digress—and show my age.)

Glossy paint is more rigid and therefore not desirable. The same with outdoor paints, which are made to flake. We usually got our flat indoor latex paint at The Home Depot. For a large labyrinth we bought two gallons of paint and mixed them together, as custom paints might vary just a little.

Our most requested color was purple. Having many partial cans of leftover purple paint, we would mix them together and call it "house purple," never to be duplicated again.

We also tried many types of painting devices. Judy was expert with the foam roller, but us ordinary mortals usually used a brush.

Arranging workers on the canvas depended on the size and number of workers. With a small labyrinth, we started in the center and worked our way outward, so as not to get into the wet paint with our feet or butts. With a larger pattern and numerous workers, we started on a middle circuit and had two groups, one working inward and the others outward.

Detailing

The difference between a professional job and amateurs is the attention to detail. So it's no surprise that going around and fixing any irregularities is called "detailing."

If the painting was really sloppy, with much going outside of the drawn lines, then it's best just to accept the more rustic look and not to worry about appearance. Otherwise, it's possible with the tip of a compass, an Exacto® knife and hard ink eraser to remove little blobs or slight encroachments into the path.

We have spilled paint onto the canvas, for which there was no solution. In one instance, we had to replace that section. With smaller spills we have turned the blobs into butterflies or vines or roses. Once, our studio cat tracked little paw prints across the canvas. We left them, much to the thrill of the elementary school that bought the labyrinth.

If painting one section at a time, let the day's work dry overnight before attempting to roll it up and move to a new spot.

Latex paint is flexible and is not bothered by folding up the canvas regularly. The paint won't crack or chip unless it was put on too thick.

Perimeter

It's best to draw and cut the perimeter of the canvas before taking it back to be hemmed. In some cases we sold blank canvas, hemmed and ready for someone to draw and paint. It was quite a bit of work to prepare, as we had to lay out the axes to measure and draw the perimeter and then take it back to be hemmed.

Transporting the labyrinth

For large labyrinths, 30' to 36' in diameter, we used wheeled Rubbermaid® tubs for storage and transportation. When we tried out the cheaper Sterilite® tubs from Walmart, we found they were not as durable and were susceptible to breaking when shipped. In the winter, the plastic gets brittle sitting in the cold UPS trucks, and even the Rubbermaid® sometimes got broken.

An old snapshot of eight 45-gallon Rubbermaid® tubs containing 36' labyrinths in one load in my old '77 Ford pickup (crew cab, 8' bed).

An alternative is to get wheeled duffle bags. The ones at Target or discount stores usually have too many compartments. All you need is one big open space. The solution: shop at a sporting goods store, like Academy, Sports Authority, or Dick's. They have suitable big open duffle bags.

If the labyrinth is in three pieces, you can use two or three duffle bags. Sometimes the two outer pieces will fit into one bag, although it will be rather heavy. We have carried labyrinths in suitcases and duffle bags and checked them as luggage. They rarely go over the fifty pound limit.

Going professional

In the event that you are interested in making canvas labyrinths as a business, I make some suggestions at the end of the book.

I'm happy to cover the subject of canvas labyrinths in a book of this length in which I have plenty of room to include as many instructions and illustrations as may be needed. After this brief introduction, let's get down to brass tacks. (An apropos euphemism, as brass tacks were used on the counter of the draper's shop to measure the length of cloth—perhaps even canvas— accurately rather than using an arm's length.)

Canvas

As mentioned, we use 72" natural untreated 100% cotton duck canvas, purchased in 100-yard rolls. One year we used almost six thousand yards.

Duck is a special kind of dense weave. It comes from the Dutch *doek*, meaning linen canvas. For centuries artists preferred linen to duck. Even today, some fine artists specializing in oil paints prefer to use linen. The great Dutch masters wanted a texture-free painting surface so they could paint with photographic-like accuracy. They used a white lead-based material that took months to build up thin layers and dry thoroughly. When finished, the canvas was stiff and smooth, ready to be painted.

These days, painters like to see texture in their paintings. In some cases, they cover the canvas with gesso, which serves as a base. I know of a few canvas labyrinths done this way, but it isn't necessary. Paint works just fine applied directly to the canvas.

Weaving in general has two movements or directions, the warp and the weft. I've seen the following illustration on several websites (*i.e.* http://www.denimbro.com). It shows single strands, whereas duck is woven with two yarns in the warp and one yarn in the weft. It's so dense that paint does not bleed through (unless it's thinned). More about paint later.

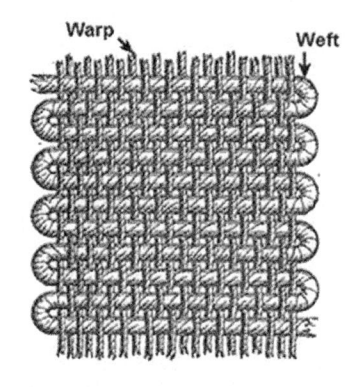

The best ducks are numbered according to their weight. The larger the number the lower the weight. We have always used #12, the lightest weight, which is between 10½ and 11½ ounces per square yard. I have seen labyrinths made from #10 cotton duck, but they are needlessly heavy.

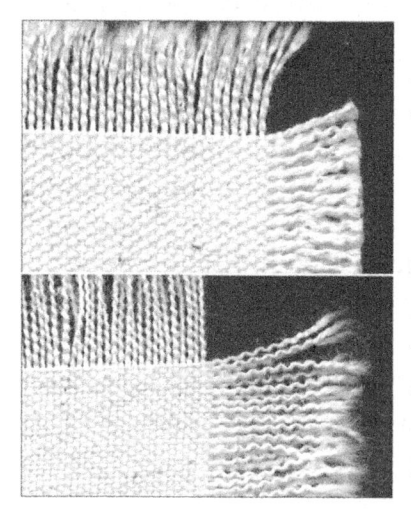

In this illustration (below left), the top fabric is #10 and the bottom #12. You can see how much less texture there is to the #12, making it easier to paint.

Being double filled (the two strands in the warp) makes the weave much denser, smoother, stiffer, and durable. The natural cotton has no chemicals added, no dyes or sizing.

It gets confusing with measuring canvas duck. The official number system is based on a piece of material 36" x 22". I've no idea why that size was chosen. To get the number, subtract the weight from 19. The #12 weighs 7 ounces for that size piece, hence 19 - 7 = 12. However, I've also seen the weight given by the square yard, 36" x 36", which is larger by almost a half, making the #12 around 10 ½ ounces.

Confused? If #1 equals 18 ounces (19 - 18 = 1), then how do they number canvas that is 19 ounces or more? It's called naught duck, naught meaning zero, heavier (smaller number) than the #1.

Duck canvas has many admirable qualities, but also a few negatives. If abraded, it can fray. When wet it can stretch or shrink or pucker up. If it gets damp and dries slowly, it's prone to mildew. Its manufacture is unkind to the environment (pesticides, water).

Some artificial fabrics may be stronger or more waterproof, but I have always preferred the natural canvas. I believe that the Labyrinth Company, which prints its canvas labyrinths mechanically, uses some kind of polycanvas. I presume it makes the ink less likely to smear or absorb.

John Ridder (www.paxworks.com) once made labyrinths on billboard vinyl but can no longer find the material. (I priced having a labyrinth printed using billboard technology, but it cost three times my retail price.) John uses polycanvas, which he describes as polyester fabric with a PVC backing. It comes only in 58" widths and must be painted twice. Not ideal in either respect.

I've experimented with nylon and some rubberized window shade material but I always come back to canvas.

Only once did I use treated canvas. It gives off an offensive odor that is especially pungent when used indoors, as fabric labyrinths generally are. I don't recommend it.

Some people have made labyrinths on tarpaulins (tarps). I once made a portable labyrinth with lines of duct tape on a 30' x 30' blue tarp. That worked quite well, but duct tape didn't come in such great colors then as are available now. The gray tape and bright blue tarp were not very subtle.

The original duct tape (used on heating and air conditioning ducts) was made from duck canvas. Is that confusing? So when people call it duck tape, they aren't wrong, historically, although the modern version is of a different composition.

Canvas is not an outdoor product (even if you waterproof it). If you are very careful you can put it on clean dry concrete and, passing birds or animals not withstanding, it might be okay. I know of several labyrinths that were not properly dried and turned black from mildew.

Forget about canvas labyrinths on grass. Even if you put a tarp under it, it's very unruly and hard to walk on. Better to just paint a temporary one on the grass than to use a portable canvas labyrinth.

Cleaning natural canvas is problematic. You could try to spray it with a protectant like ScotchGard®, but the best policy is to keep it clean. Remove shoes (or wear disposable paper shoe covers, bought in the paint section of the hardware store) when walking. Barefoot isn't ideal, due to body oils. We always have some clean white socks available when people walk.

In the days when we rented canvas labyrinths, these things were strictly forbidden on the labyrinth:
- shoes
- candles
- food or drink

Not everyone obeyed our rules. We tried every kind of way to clean canvas and found no chemicals to be satisfactory. They removed the stain but left a bigger one of their own. Wax can be removed by using the old paper bag and iron trick, but the color from the dye often remains. Vacuuming and sweeping (using a clean, dedicated broom) help. We remove small spots with a soft white eraser.

I had a nightmare about taking a canvas labyrinth to a rug cleaning establishment. When I picked it up, it was a blank piece of canvas. They proudly bragged, "We got all that paint off for you." Ugh!

Single filled canvas and army canvas are not the same density and do not hold paint as well. Canvas duck, because of its stiffness, lies flat. Nylon (parachute material), sheets, drop cloths, lighter materials of all kinds wrinkle and move and make it almost dangerous to walk (tripping hazard).

Feel free to experiment. If you find a material superior to canvas, let me know.

Where to get canvas

When ordering canvas, allow for a little space between the intended labyrinth pattern and the edge of the canvas. If you use 72" canvas as we did, then the canvas may be 24' (less a few inches for hemming and seams) but the pattern will be closer to 23' or even less. Similarly, our 36' canvas had a pattern just under 35' in diameter.

When writing this section, I went to the websites of my two normal suppliers and found very little about #12 cotton duck. I'm sure you could order it. They are:

Trivantage (www.trivantage.com)
C. R. Daniels (www.crdaniels.com)

While on the internet, I found some other sources that I haven't tried but that look good. Most vendors sell canvas to artists in very small sizes at a high price. The largest size I found was 58" wide and six yards long. Six yards is only eighteen feet, which would be a small labyrinth. Plus, you would need to have four panels, which would require excessive sewing.

Instead of art supply purveyors, look for discount sellers. I once looked into ordering directly from India (such as http://www.indiamart.com/srisenthil-andavar-textiles/cotton-fabrics.htmlw), but the minimum order (in one case, 10,000 yards) and the need to find a safe dry place to store it discouraged me.

The company you get to do your sewing may have good connections for buying canvas wholesale (if they don't mark it up too much). Such is the case for the Mickleys, below.

Mickley's Canvas Products

These are my friends in St. Louis whom I mentioned earlier. They are hard working and reliable. They will do the sewing for you and give you the canvas at a good price. It may be cheaper to get it from them and pay for some shipping that to use other sources. At one time, I was their largest single customer. Here is their contact information again.

Mickley's Canvas Products, 9523 Watson Industrial Park, St. Louis, Missouri 63126. Tel: (314) 963-0800. They don't seem to have a website.

Canvas-fabrics.com and Sailrite

Canvas has been used for sails for hundreds of years. At sailrite you can buy sail kits. This is a source of waterproofed and treated canvas. I've always wanted to make a canvas labyrinth and then glue it to a concrete pad outdoors, perhaps varnishing over it, just to see how well it would last. Marine canvas is used for boat covers, intended to be out in the weather. If you really must use your canvas labyrinth outdoors, consider this material. It's quite heavy. This site included the following information, which I found interesting. The rating system is one (worst) to 5 (best).

Cotton Duck (Marine-treated, preshrunk)

Cotton duck, often called Otis Permasol, Vivatex or Sunforger, is an all cotton duck with special marine finish. Allow about an extra 3% for shrinkage under normal usage. Soft hand ideal for outdoor covers where low cost is important. Use for winter boat covers, boat deck canvassing, awnings, drop cloths, bags and hats. Available in many weights and thread deniers.

<u>Breathe Ability (5):</u> Although a tight weave, cotton duck allows for excellent passage of moisture through the material.

<u>Waterproof (4):</u> When cotton duck gets saturated, the fibers will swell and the openings in the weave close making the fabric nearly waterproof. Cotton duck will shrink some over time even if it undergoes a "preshrinking" process.

<u>Abrasion Resistance (4):</u> Heavier versions are quite abrasion resistant as the fabric is soft and forms well to harsh surfaces and corners.

<u>UV Resistance (1):</u> The main disadvantage of cotton duck is that it fails quickly when exposed to harsh sun. Some improvement has been made by applying chemical treatments to the fabric but it is still inferior to almost all of the synthetic alternatives.

<u>Colorfastness (N/A):</u> Cotton fabrics take and hold dye very well. For most all outdoor applications this fabric is sold in a natural or pearl grey color. Low pricing is generally the appeal and bright colors are not readily available.

<u>Clean Ability (4):</u> Easy to clean and wash dirt free from the crevasses of the yarns.

http://canvas-fabrics.com/Marine-treated-preshrunk-Cotton-Duck/index.htm
http://www.sailrite.com/Cotton-Duck#!Cotton-Duck

Many fabric distributors cater to the awning industry. They will offer Sunbrella® and other colorful outdoor fabrics. I've found them to be very expensive and not well-suited for making labyrinths.

BigDuckCanvas.com

From their website:

Numbered ducks are identified by the "#" sign in front of a number from 1 to 12. This plied yarn weave makes for a tighter and stronger weave construction over single fill ducks and are used for more rugged outdoor or industrial applications.

Numbered ducks will vary in weight from mill to mill and there is no real universal standard weight for each number. We have included our ounce weight per square yard in our product descriptions to lessen the confusion.

#12 is our lightest weight numbered duck at 11.5 oz per square yard and #1 is the heaviest at 30 oz. Anything heavier than a #1 would would be considered a Naught Duck. As if it wasn't confusing enough, we also carry Army Duck which is technically a numbered duck as well but uses smaller plied yarns to produce a finer texture and better strength.

Hm-m-m-m-m. That Army Duck sounds interesting. It might be worth checking out. I suspect it will not have the body of #12 duck and not lie as flat, but it might be worth a look.

Order Quantity	Price per yard
10-24 yards	$6.75
25-49 yards	$6.00
50-99 yards	$5.25
100 + yards	$4.50

These are extremely good prices. I used to pay far more than this, even with one hundred yard rolls.

See: www.bigduckcanvas.com

Allen's Canvas

This source has a great selection of widths. www.allenscanvas.com/100%20yd%20rolls.html. I used to pay over $15 a yard for 144" canvas.

> #12 Cotton Duck Canvas
> 48" #12 100 yds. $3.85 per. yd.
> 60" #12 100 yds. $4.62 per. yd.
> 72" #12 100 yds. $5.99 per. yd.
> 84" #12 100 yds. $5.82 per yd.
> 96" #12 100 yds. $6.99 per. yd.
> 120" #12 55 yds. $9.25 per yd.
> 144" #12 55 yds. $11.52 per yd.

Let's suppose that you're making a smaller labyrinth, say 24' in diameter. You could order 96" canvas (eight feet) and use three panels.

I find 144" canvas very impressive—a vast expanse of uninterrupted canvas. We didn't use it because it's very unwieldy (rolls can weigh 300 pounds), and in a few cases, not as good quality. We used 72" panels, which means two had to be sewn together to form one 12' panel. That wasn't a problem, as the folks who did our sewing (the Mickleys) had the right equipment and were very skilled. However, my colleagues tell me they all use 144" canvas.

Our 36' canvas Chartres labyrinths were made in three panels connected with Velcro®, thereby making them easier to transport (see below). Conveniently, each panel was 12' wide, the width of the 144" canvas.

Warehouse of Fabrics

This supplier gets an honorable mention. They have good prices but I didn't find rolls of #12.
http://warehousefabricsinc.com/CD7NAL.html#prodbox

Remember that #12 can be called 7 ounce (for the 36" x 22" piece weight) or 10½ ounce and sometimes even 11½ ounce (for one square yard). If you concentrate on ordering #12, you can't go far wrong.

Using Velcro®

Our 36-foot painted canvas labyrinths weighed approximately one hundred pounds. For ease of transportation, we divided the labyrinth into three pieces, which were joined by Velcro®. By making three pieces, the labyrinth became much more manageable for moving around.

Our earlier manual suggested a butt joint for the canvas sections, made possible by mixing the use of two-inch and one-inch-wide Velcro®. With that system, the two-inch Velcro® is sewn face up to the bottom of one section so that it protrudes by one inch. The corresponding one-inch Velcro® is sewn on the bottom of the adjacent panel, so that it fits onto the protruding one inch of the first panel. As a result, the edges of the canvas do not overlap, they butt edge to edge.

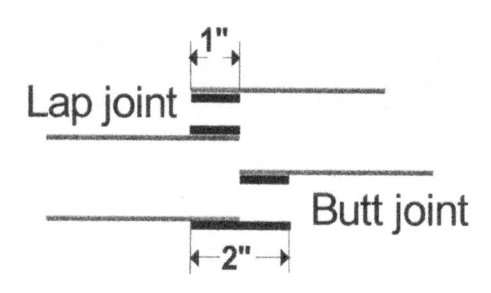

For several months we conducted a campaign to find ways of making the canvas lay as flat as possible, eliminating most of the wrinkles. Some of the wrinkles are caused by the selvedge edge of the canvas, which is drawn up slightly to prevent unraveling. By drawing up the edges slightly, the centers of the panels have a bit of looseness to them, which causes small wrinkles. That appears to be the nature of canvas, which we will have to accept.

There were some things, however, we were able to do with the sewing, to keep the labyrinth as flat as possible. Using a single overlap and double-needle machines for the seams, for example. It turned out that the mixed Velcro® system was causing quite a bit of wrinkling. When we switched to a simple lap joint, using all one-inch Velcro®, many of the wrinkles disappeared. With the lap joint, the Velcro® is sewn face up on the top of the bottom piece, and face down on the bottom of the top piece. Got that? Fewer wrinkles are a far greater advantage, in my mind, for the slightly bulkier lap joint.

Large labyrinth in three sections.

It's generally easier to lay out the center piece first, and then connect the outer pieces, which we call "wings." If the center piece has the Velcro® arranged with hook on one edge and loop on the other (sewn on top of the canvas, face up), then each wing will be different, one with hook and one with loop. As a result, the labyrinth can only be assembled in one way.

Once the pattern is drawn and painted, putting together the labyrinth is not hard, as the pieces only fit together one way and the pattern lines up with itself.

When connecting the sections, start at the center and work outward. The first time you do this, prior to drawing the labyrinth, it's very important to keep the same tension on both the top and bottom pieces, because once you have drawn the pattern, the labyrinth will always have to be connected in the same way. If there is looseness in either piece, it will cause wrinkling.

For churches that don't transport the labyrinth, we have found it convenient to leave the pieces hooked together and to fold the whole labyrinth. It's heavy, but just put the storage tub on its side and roll the labyrinth into it. Then it's just a matter of pulling it upright and wheeling it away. John Ridder sews many of his 36' labyrinths into one piece, eliminating the bulky Velcro® and the hassle of using it.

Pay attention to the direction of the seams and Velcro®. I like the seams to be horizontal (perpendicular to the entrance path). Otherwise, there will be a seam directly on the vertical axis, which goes right up the entrance path and into the middle. Walking along a seam in bare feet can be uncomfortable.

The same applies with the Velcro®. A lumpy Velcro® seam right up the center of the path is not desirable. This won't be the case if you have three sections, such as a Chartres pattern. But suppose you are making a 24' pattern, using 12' canvas, and doing the sewing yourself. Rather than sewing a seam (to make a single piece of cloth), you could sew Velcro® onto the edge and have a two-piece labyrinth.

Unfortunately, that will put the bulky Velcro® right up the vertical axis again. Even if the seams went the other way (horizontal), they would still go right through the center. For this reason we usually make any canvas 24' or smaller one integral unit rather than two pieces.

Storage tub

We supplied a large plastic Rubbermaid® bin that holds the entire labyrinth, as well as canvas bags that allow one to transport each section separately. If you have one of these bins, there's a secret in how to move it without straining your back.

Rather than dragging it behind you, stand it up so it's resting on its side. Then tip it slightly toward you and push it in front of you. The weight remains mostly on the wheels, and not your back.

Left: Wrong way. Don't drag it (no weight on the wheels)
Right: The correct way, push it in front of you. Thanks, Judy.

John Ridder tells me he buys 45-gallon bins similar to what you see in the photographs at Lowes (Centrex Plastics, LLC, Rugged Tote with latching lid, Item/model #314131, $29.98).

Folding canvas

When folding the canvas labyrinth, the final size or shape doesn't matter much. It should fit your storage requirements. The first step, however, is very important: Fold the labyrinth in half, so that the top painted surface faces itself and the bottom side of the canvas is outward. That will protect the painted surface from getting dirty. If you have a broom handy, you can sweep off the bottom of the canvas as you fold it up.

We developed a clever way for one person to fold the canvas in half. I call it the parachute method. Stand on the canvas near the edge, facing the direction in which you want to fold. Pick up the edge of the canvas behind you up to shoulder height. You will be looking away from it. Then run toward the other side, holding your hands high. The canvas will catch air and billow up behind you (hence the parachute moniker). Just before reaching the other side let go. The canvas will waft back down to the floor. With only a little straightening and adjusting it should be folded in half, as desired.

Rolling the canvas is not a good idea until it has been folded in half. Otherwise you will roll dirt from the back onto the front, which is not ideal. If you want to roll it up, do it after first folding the canvas in half. (Exception: rolling up canvas for a painting table.) We just keep folding it until it's small enough to handle.

The sections of our 36-foot canvas are twelve feet wide, with a seam down the middle (since the section is made from two 6-foot-wide panels, sewn together). If you fold that section exactly in half along the seam, the seam gets some rather funky bends and hitches. Instead, fold it just short of being exactly in half, by an inch or two, so that the fold isn't right on the seam.

John Ridder tells me he rarely uses Velcro® as it is so bulky and hard to walk on. He makes the large canvases in a single piece. It may take two people to move it, but that's a small inconvenience for the easy of unfolding it without having to join all that Velcro®.

Storing canvas

I've seen some churches that fold the labyrinth in half and then roll it up and keep it up against the wall (or in one case, on the stage in the meeting hall).

We used to have piles of canvas scraps in our first studio. When we moved, we gave it away by the van load. In the process, we found that the mice had turned it into a rodent apartment house. In one case we had something eat right through the plastic to get inside a container.

In addition to storage bins we used to send along canvas bags (made from scraps). In that way, each bag could be carried separately and thrown into the truck of a car. We tried shipping the labyrinth in bags once, but they got incredibly dirty. Plus, Fed Ex lost one of the three bags.

When the canvas sits for a long time, the folds and wrinkles may become pronounced, but they should relax once it's laid out. If not, you can always stretch it a bit using the system we describe in this book.

On this labyrinth, you can see the seam going up the middle of the path. That's not how we usually did it. using 144" canvas will eliminate that.

You can also see how the canvas puckers a little from the painting. That's one reason we stretch it, to minimize that effect.

Tools

Mechanical pencils

For writing on canvas I use the gripper type of mechanical pencil. It has a long lead inside which advances by loosening a gripper mechanism operated by the button on the top. This is called a "clutch" mechanical pencil.

The leads are rated by an HB scale, which stands for hardness and blackness. If you use a hard lead it will be very light, which is good if you need to erase it on canvas, but will be hard to follow when painting. We use HB (equivalent to a #2 pencil) or 2B (softer, darker, can draw with a very light touch.) It takes practice to draw without breaking the lead. Our floor had some irregular places that always caused us to break the leads until we memorized where they were and slowed down when we reached them.

The pencils make a noise when you draw. The faster you go, the higher the pitch. At the annual gathering of the Labyrinth Society in 2002, I gave a talk about my life as a labyrinth maker entitled "Screaming Pencils." That's when you know things are going well (when the pencils scream, not when giving a talk).

You will also need erasers. We use the soft white kind. When walking on the labyrinth, avoid stepping on the drawn lines as you can smudge them. When painting, cover the line, so it won't show.

Stretching the canvas

The tools for making a canvas labyrinth can be quite simple. First, it's necessary to hold the canvas down and stretch it slightly to eliminate as many wrinkles as possible, as they make drawing difficult. We use elastic Bungee® cords for this purpose. One end is attached to the canvas and the other to something heavy.

At most big box hardware stores you can get tarp clips which attach to the edge of the canvas. If the canvas is too thin for it to get a good grip, just fold it over to a double thickness. Nicely, they have a hole in them, through which we can insert the hook of a Bungee® cord.

Our studio had a wooden floor. It was tempting to screw some kind of cleat to the floor to receive the other end of the stretch cords, but instead we used 35-pound dumbbells. For our larger labyrinths, such as the Chartres pattern, we used sixteen dumbbells. For smaller canvases we use eight. Moving 560 pounds of heavy iron is quite an exercise. We stored them in a wooden chest on wheels.

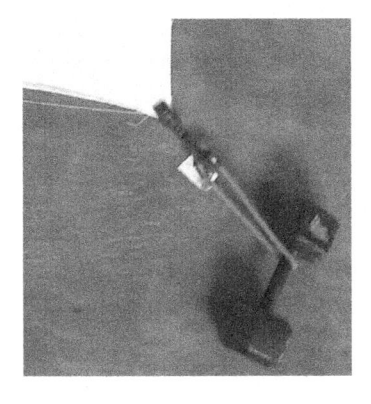

Canvas, tarp clip, Bungee® cord, dumbbell.

You could use other heavy things such as cinder blocks or folding tables. In a pinch, you can pull the canvas tight and tape it to the floor using a kind of tape that doesn't leave residue (see next section).

Masking Tape

Only a few kinds of masking tape can be removed without leaving residue. One is painter's tape, typically blue, but it has very little stick to it. I've found that it comes up at inopportune times.

Frog Tape (green, in a plastic container) is a bit better. If you are only using the tape to keep the canvas from moving and to mark a few start/stop lines on the canvas, then Frog Tape should be fine. However, if you plan to tape the lines for the whole labyrinth (discussed shortly), you will need to order a tape made by 3M Company called "231." Catchy name.

It has a very good tack and still removes cleanly. We use it outdoors on concrete and it survives rain (even though the spec sheet says it's an indoor tape). The 231A masking tape works just as well. I believe it was developed for the aerospace industry. Since the tape is made to withstand bake cycles, it works well outdoors in hot weather without getting gooey. Here's the official description.

Scotch® Performance Masking Tape 231/231A is a premium high performance crepe paper masking tape designed to perform well in most industrial painting situations, including the use of bake cycles. This smooth to the touch masking tape, embodies all the features that are desirable of a paint masking tape and designed specifically for the professional painter.

I have my 231 shipped to me from Budnick Converting (see http://www.budnick.com/Datasheets/3M/231). When I lived in St. Louis, they were just across the river in Illinois. What are they converting you might ask? They buy the tape in long logs and then cut it to the width you want. I usually get 1" and 2" widths. The tape is not cheap, costing almost $8 per roll for the 1" and $15 for the 2". If you want to be a professional and want to get the best results, take care to use the best tools.

As you might suspect, you can get 231 on Amazon.com: http://www.amazon.com/Scotch-Paint-Masking-231-231A. Here is their description of it:

Rubber adhesive provides instant adhesion and resists lifting or curling for sharp paint lines

Smooth mini-crepe paper backing conforms and maintains integrity when formed around a corner

Backing is easy to tear resists slivering and provides one piece removal

Controlled unwind dispenses evenly and is less likely to tear off roll

Backing is heat resistant for high-temperature paint bake cycles, up to 300° F/ 149° C

Straightedge

Depending on the size of the labyrinth, it's important to have a rigid straightedge (not a tape measure) from 6' to 12' or even longer. We had an 18' straightedge that we made from aluminum awning channel. I also bought a very precise 12' straight edge online.

Here's the thing. You don't need the straightedge for making measurements. We can do that with a tape measure. However, there are some fancy graphics straightedges that have a measuring scale on them, if you are so inclined.

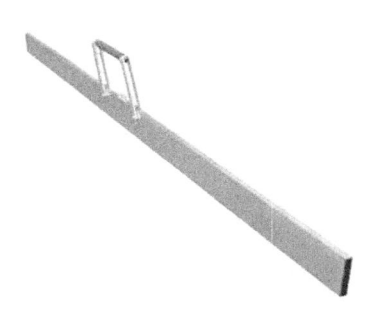

I looked around and found a device for testing whether asphalt is level (left). It's aluminum, ½" x 3" x 12', with a carrying handle, which would need to be removed. You can find it here:

http://store.sealcoating.com/asphalt-highway-paving-straight edge-checking-tool---12-ft-handle-p523.aspx

Me using a long straightedge to lay out a labyrinth pattern. After lining it up, I lay down a row of masking tape beside it (in this case marking out the entrances).

I have made straightedges by taping together several shorter ones. The problem is that the tape gets in the way when trying to draw a straight line. If you are just laying down masking tape, however, it works fine. If you have some mechanical capability, you could buy three 72" straightedges. Put two of them end to end and the third on top, in the middle. Tape them securely (temporarily) and then drill several holes through the double thickness.

Use small bolts with tapered heads and counter sink them so the head is even with the straightedge. That will be the bottom. The rest of the bolts and the nuts will stick out the top. The benefit of this design is that you can disassemble the straightedge for easier traveling. You could even use shorter straightedges, such as 48" and use more of them. You could carry them in a case made for a 48" level.

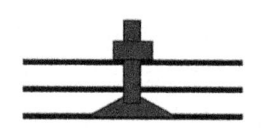

Above: Three straight edges, two on the bottom, one on top

Left: Detail of bolt attaching two straightedges (head at bottom, nut at top)

In a dire emergency or noncritical situations, two people can hold a piece of masking tape at each end and carefully line it up before sticking it down. It makes a reasonably straight line, especially for a temporary labyrinth. For more exacting results, you will need a straightedge of some kind.

Layout the pattern

We will make a center post and a compass, but first, we need access to the center point of the labyrinth to lay out certain measurements for the pattern. All of these can be done with masking tape. Here are some possibilities, depending on the pattern:

1. Mark the center of the canvas (if a circular pattern) or multiple center points (if a classical pattern).

2. Lay out the vertical and horizontal axes.

3. Lay out the location of the entrance paths so you don't extend the circles where they don't need to be.

4. Lay out the center point for all circles or arcs, including turns, line ends, and lunations.

5. Put a piece of tape down the vertical axis and mark on it the spacing for the circles. By making the marks on the tape, later you can remove the tape and no marks will be left showing on the canvas.

6. Lay out the location for the petal crosses of a Chartres labyrinth.

7. Lay out marks for the desired perimeter (square, octagon, etc. These can also be done after the circles are made and the weights removed.

There could be other measurements for which you will need access to the center point(s). When they are complete, you are ready for the next step.

Center Post

Before we make a compass, we need a center post. I use a pipe mounted on a piece of wood, held down by two or three 44-pound Olympic barbell weights. Specifically, I cut a square piece of ¾" plywood around 14" on the side. I draw two diagonal lines from opposite corners to find the center point. With a 1" paddle drill, I make a hole in the center (to be explained momentarily).

Or, rather than making your own center board, buy one at a hobby shop made for decoupage, which has finished edges. Find the center and drill the hole.

Next, buy a ¾" pipe flange and screw it to the board, centered over the hole. Into the pipe flange you screw a pipe of the desired height (I make mine 8" to 12"). Then put two or three heavy weights over the pipe, to keep the center from moving. I don't mean little wimpy plastic-covered ten-pounders. I mean serious Olympic weights, with large center holes, that weigh forty-four pounds each. In some cases I use two, in other cases, three.

Center post made of wooden base, flange, and pipe

Look through the hole to see your center mark and place the board there. Then carefully add one weight, screw in the pipe and add the remaining weights. Voila, a center.

Compass

My basic compass utilizes an ordinary yardstick (http://www.dickblick.com/products/griffin-yardstick-compass/). This clever device consists of a slotted pencil and point made to slide onto a standard size yardstick. By that I mean the "thin" kind. There are also thick yardsticks which won't fit into the slots. You can tape two yardsticks together and make a circle up to eleven feet in diameter.

Yardstick compass.

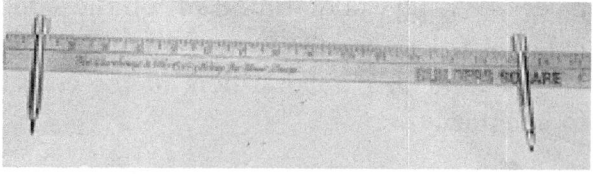

Drawing a line for painting we need to make two circles, an inner one and an outer one, between which we paint the line. You can do this in one fell swoop by putting two pencils on the yardstick and drawing two lines at once, in parallel. (Any mistakes are also doubled.)

We also need a large compass, capable of making circles up to 36' in diameter. Yes, you could go bigger, but I don't think it's a good idea, as the canvas will be unreasonably heavy. Even a 36' canvas only fits in a few large spaces, such as gymnasiums or meeting halls without pillars.

The big circle compass is made of several parts.

1. A piece of yardstick with two pencils mounted on it, one line's width apart.

2. The weighted center post, as previously described.

3. A tape measure. We won't be using it to measure anything. It's handy because it's lightweight and won't stretch the way rope does.

4. Two clamps to clamp the piece of yardstick to the tape measure.

I put a threaded cap on the top of the center pipe, into which I drill a hole and fasten a thin threaded bolt, putting nuts both inside and outside the cap to hold it in place. Over the thin bolt I put the end of my tape measure.

Most tape measures end in a little hook so you can catch the end of a board or corner of a wall when measuring. I use a pliers and straighten out this hook and then, if there isn't one, drill a hole in it. I insert the hole through the bolt on top of the pipe. The tape measure should swivel freely with very little excess movement.

The tape measure has a clip for carrying on one's belt. Instead, I slide it onto the end of the piece of yardstick to which the pencils are attached. Three small quick-release clamps secure the yardstick to the tape measure.

Place the pencils on the marks indicating the location of the circles, clamp the yardstick to the tape measure, check it again for any small adjustments, and draw the circle. Keep a slight outward pressure to keep the tape measure taut. Keep the piece of yardstick in line with the tape measure. Start and stop the circles at predesignated spots.

Judy could draw at a continuous walking pace. I draw part of an arc, then move forward, draw more of the arc, and proceed thusly.

When finished, remove the clamps, line up the pencils to the next circle mark, clamp them down, and draw again. Repeat for all circles. If you have a pattern with interior turns (sometimes called labryses), you will want to stop the circle where the line ends for the turn(s). It's easiest to mark these out in advance before drawing each circle.

With just a little practice and a steady hand, one can learn to draw accurate circles.

Here is our compass (above), with center post, weights, tape measure, pencils, and clamps. The upward point at the end of the yardstick is to hold the tape measure in place, as it goes through the slot. Instead of quick release clamps you can also use spring clamps.

Judy Hopen was such a precise painter that we always drew our canvas labyrinths in pencil, and then she would paint them by hand. For other workers, however, we used our fancy dancy tape machine and taped the pattern to the canvas.

Notice that the tape machine lays down two parallel strips of tape, the equivalent of using two pencils to draw dual lines.

The tape machine is sometimes called a Line or Game Taping Machine. I bought ours from SealMaster: (http://www.sealmaster.net/Tools%20an%20Accessories.shtml).

Dual taping machine in action.

For such serious equipment, a tape measure would never do for the arm. We need something rigid. SealMaster also sells a kit with pipes that screw together to make the rigid arm. However, the way the tape machine connects to the pipes was not suitable for labyrinths. So I had to custom make a bracket for the tape machine and a multi-directional swivel for the center.

Approaching the center, the circles get smaller and the angle of the arm changes. To accommodate the changing angle, I made my bracket from a large strap hinge, which has free movement to change as needed.

The center swivel must allow for adjusting the length of the arm as well as swiveling in a circle and up and down. If you really need to make such a device, write to me and I'll share my designs. Eventually I will write an instruction manual for contractors and professional labyrinth makers that will include such tips.

The taping machine makes easy work of laying out the labyrinth circles. For the smaller details, such as turns, petals, and lunations, we draw them first and then tape along the lines. We are careful to always have the drawn line showing (not covering it with tape) so that it will be covered when the pattern is painted.

Left: Lars Howlett and Lea Goode-Harris aligning the tape machine to their circle spacing marks to lay out a labyrinth on a wooden floor. My center swivel goes up and down as well as turning. Note how the length of the arm is adjustable.

Taped and partially painted canvas labyrinth.

If you don't want to spend almost a thousand dollars for this kind of equipment, you can draw the pattern first in pencil and then mask it off by hand. It takes a little while, but the painting goes very fast.

In such case, it's important to press the tape down to avoid getting paint under it. This is made harder by the texture of the canvas. I've made many experimental devices for this purpose, but the best one turns out to be the back of a large serving spoon. Below are some other candidates.

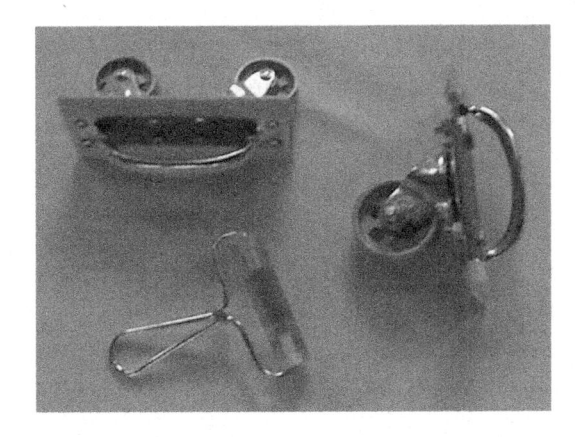

Dollies

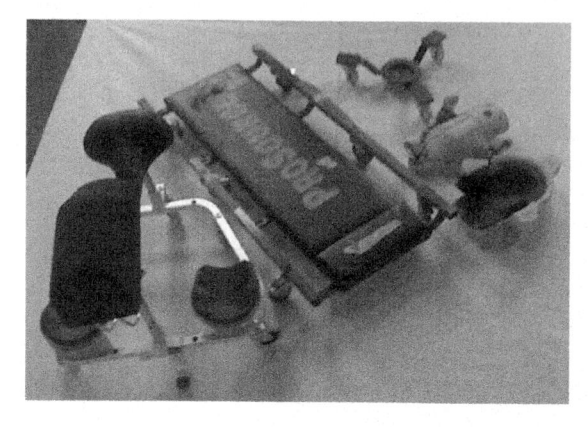

When drawing and painting, moving around can take effort. We used several types of dollies for "transportation" around the canvas.

In the middle of the photo is a standard mechanic's dolly of the type used to roll under a vehicle. Judy would draw the lunations in a Chartres pattern, lying on her stomach on the dolly, propelling herself with her toes. To the right are knee blades. That's right, knee pads with wheels. You can really zip along. In the back is a standard three-wheeled dolly, onto which we put a sitting cushion. On the left is a Racatac dolly.

Here is a better picture of the Racatac without the chest rest. Sit on the seat then kneel forward. You can get them at numerous places on the internet, including www.racatac.com.

The dollies were used exclusively on the canvas, to keep the wheels clean.

Templates

Depending on the pattern, you may need templates to draw the labyrinth design on canvas. For some, it may only be a half circle to draw the line ends. For a Chartres labyrinth, you will need three different templates, for the petals, the line ends, and the lunations. They are covered in great detail in our other book, *Chartres Labyrinth: Construction Manual*. Here's a brief summary.

The line end is just a half circle. The key is to make it a little smaller than the line width as you will be drawing around it, slightly enlarging the size of the template. Sometimes I make the line end template at the bottom of the petal template, giving it a dual purpose.

I draw the lunations in a clockwise direction. The notch in the left side of the template allows me to see the previous lunation circle that I just drew, so I can determine the proper width for the tooth.

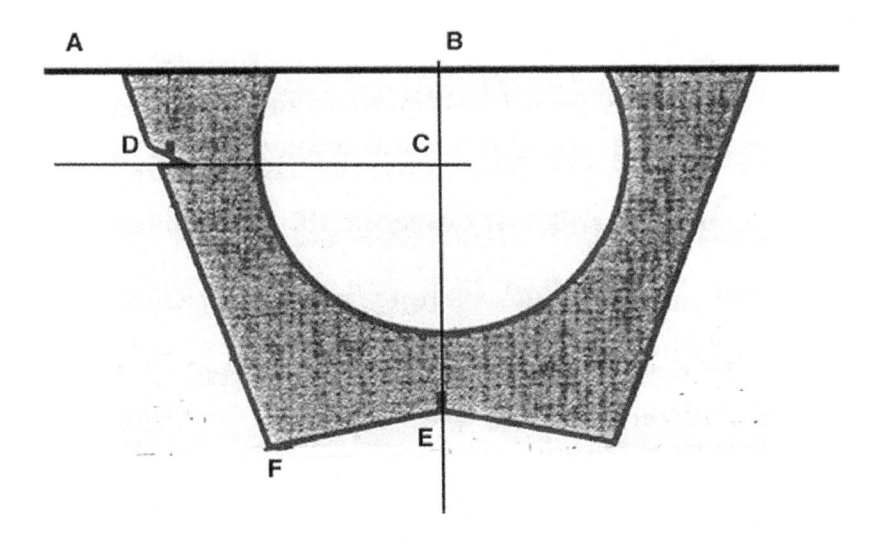

Following are directions in how to make this template.

A: Top of tooth
The horizontal line labeled "A" represents the edge of the template material, be it cardboard or polycarbonate or sheet metal. The top of the template, along the line A, is where we will draw the tops of the teeth.

B: First vertical
The first step in making the template is to draw the vertical line that will serve as the central axis. If using poster board for a temporary pattern (for a single labyrinth), I usually use ballpoint pen or a fine marker. On plastic or metal, I use a Sharpie®. A T-square works best for this.

C: Center of circle
To draw the lunation circle, we have to determine where the center is. Note that from point B to the lunation circle, measured down the vertical axis, represents the height of the tooth. Point C is determined by the difference between the tooth height and the lunation circle radius.

D: Locating the tooth width notch
Draw a line perpendicular to the vertical axis from point C. Since that means it's parallel to the top of the material, you can just measure down the same distance as for point C and connect the two points. In this notch you can see the previously drawn circle. With a mark on the template, you can keep the teeth to a uniform width. It's necessary to fudge a little when making lunations. When setting the template to the correct tooth width, it may not be directly over the spacing mark. Draw the first half of the lunation circle and then move the template to the mark before drawing the second half. In that way, the variation is in the circle rather than the tooth and is much harder to notice.

E: Determining line width
The distance from the bottom of the lunation circle to point E represents the width of the twelfth circle. This template is used

on the inside of the twelfth circle as the outer circle will be the lunations.

F: Template corners

There is no specific measurement for making the bottom edge of the template. This is how I do it, but you can make it any shape that you choose. The corners help to line up the template properly.

When I first started making canvas labyrinths my assistant was Karen Weiss. She became a successful real estate agent and later opened her own yoga studio. This is the only photo I have of her working on a labyrinth.

She's drawing lunations with a template such as I've just described. When I draw lunations, I don't do the splits.

The Petal Template

The petal template is not just a standard cross. The illustration shows the proportions and arrangement of the circles. The bottom of the template is the width of the line (minus a little, to allow for tracing). It is here you can put a half circle for the line ends. I make a straight line down the middle of the template to assure proper alignment with the center of the labyrinth (for which I use a straightedge). The exceptions to the rule are the partial crosses at the entrance, which are parallel to the entrance path and do not point toward the center.

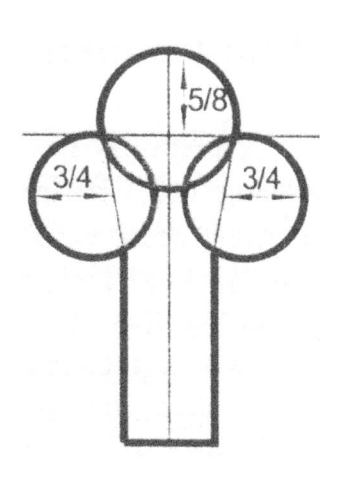

Painting

Painting canvas labyrinths is within the reach of any steady-handed person, given a few hints. However, it does take a long time. The lines in a labyrinth are longer than most people realize. Having painted almost one thousand canvas labyrinths, we still took thirty to thirty-five hours to paint a large one. For the inexperienced, that time may be considerably more. That means you must have a place to draw and paint the labyrinth for at least a week. Alternately, you can draw it, and then paint it elsewhere one section at a time.

Paint

For paint, use indoor, flat, latex house paint, like you would use to paint a room inside your house (we get ours at The Home Depot). Flat is important because semi-gloss or high-gloss paints get the gloss by having harder surfaces, which would be more brittle and prone to crack. Indoor is better than outdoor paint, as the latter has extra chemicals designed to flake slightly to endure weather.

To paint a 35-foot Chartres pattern we buy two gallons of paint, and usually have some left. We mix them together to guarantee a consistent color. Smaller labyrinths obviously take less paint. Our 24-foot Santa Rosa labyrinth takes less than a gallon, and our 12-foot personal labyrinth takes about a quart. The labyrinth looks big, but you are only painting the lines, not the path. One coat is sufficient.

If the paint seems thick and it's hard to get a straight and accurate edge, consider adding some Floetrol®, a paint additive used for spray painting latex paint. Latex cannot be thinned with water—use Floetrol® instead. It breaks down the surface tension and allows the paint to flow more smoothly.

I did a little experiment to see how much Floetrol® can be added. When I got up to fifty percent, it made the paint became almost pearlescent and somewhat transparent. It also became thin enough to soak through the canvas duck. Best to follow the manufacturer's instructions.

The color that you choose can also effect the ease of painting. For some reason, we have always found red to be a difficult color. In general, the darker the color the better. Bright colors tend to vibrate. Light colors not only don't cover as well, lapping is far more noticeable.

Lapping occurs when you stop painting long enough for the paint to dry. When you resume, taking up where you left off, you are obliged to overlap the dry paint slightly with the new wet paint, so there is no gap. This gives that small area of overlap two coats of paint, which has a slightly different (darker) color or appearance than a single coat.

One way to avoid this is to put a piece of masking tape where you want to stop. Pick a narrow spot, such as a line, rather than in the middle of a petal or labrys. Paint right up onto the masking tape.

When resuming painting the next day, remove the masking tape and put a new piece across the end of the painted line with only a hair's breadth of overlap. This makes it much less obvious.

Similarly, it's not good to try to touch up thin areas unless they are really bad, as the double coating will be very apparent.

Tools

I've tried every imaginable painting tool, both mechanical and power-operated. Ultimately, I decided that the best tool is . . . a paintbrush. It holds the most paint, is easiest to control, and gives a good line. I prefer a 1½-inch, slanted, good quality brush. At The Home Depot they are locked in a cabinet. Go ahead, spend eight or ten bucks for a paintbrush. You will also need some small artist's brushes to get into the fine corners.

The only other tool to compare with the paintbrush is a small, yellow, two-inch-wide foam roller (see drawing, left). This produces a well-defined edge (as opposed to wall rollers, which are ill-defined).

Judy Hopen was a master of the foam roller. She even did line ends and petal circles with them. It was terrifying to watch her. She found that many of the rollers come with a wobble to them. They just aren't made for this kind of precision. We bought a dozen at a time and threw away half of them. We experimented with spinning them on a drill press and trimming them with a razor knife, which helped.

Use a plastic shoe box or similar container to hold your paint can and brush. I put the paint into empty plastic sorbet cans, which have tight-fitting lids (holding about a cup of paint). A Tupperware® container or refrigerator storage container would also work well. Put that container inside the shoe box. Thus, if you drip or spill, it will be inside the shoe box. You can also put your paintbrush down inside the box.

Never, I say NEVER balance your brush across the top of your paint container when you want to stop painting for a moment. It's easily knocked off, perhaps onto the canvas. Just stand it up in the corner of the plastic shoe box. When you are finished painting, you can wash out the plastic shoe box with no difficulty.

If using a foam roller, use a small half-size tray, resting on a larger flat serving tray. Be sure to avoid getting paint on the bottom of your tray or shoebox by getting too close to the line you are painting, which would make a mess.

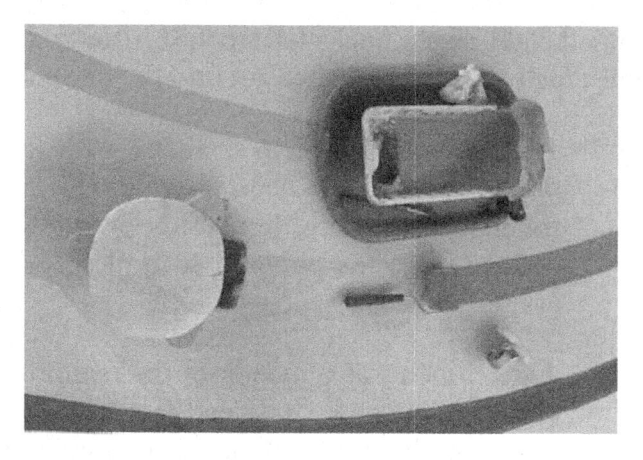

Serving tray, small paint tray, sponge roller. On the left is a three-wheeled dolly with a cushion for sitting, easily moving backwards while painting. The lines are different shades in the photo because the were rainbow colors.

Painting

As a result of cutting the perimeter of our portable labyrinths, we have many canvas scraps. Whenever we work with new painters, we have them try out on a practice piece. This is especially important with volunteers. After you see their skill level, you may wish to ask them to fix lunch instead. If you are lacking steady-handed workers, perhaps you should consider taping the pattern.

Roll one edge, and then the other. Most rollers wobble, which makes it hard.

Start in an obscure place on the labyrinth, such as the fifth or sixth line on the upper right-hand side, away from the entrance. As you gain expertise, work your way to the more visible areas, the entrance and the center. My experience is that the least talented painter goes right to the most important areas.

You can paint the Chartres labyrinth in a smaller room by painting one section at a time (see photo on p. 12). In order for the labyrinth sections which were painted separately to line up correctly when assembled, be sure to stay within the lines when at the edge of the canvas where the pattern will continue on the next piece (which is somewhat difficult, due to the bump made by the Velcro®). Otherwise, when you put the sections together the lines will be different widths and won't match up.

If you have several people working, you can start with the fifth or sixth circle and have one person work outward while another works inward. Doing this in each quadrant, you can get as many as eight people painting at the same time without interfering with each other. Four or five people might be more manageable, however.

Having learned to paint with both my left and right hand, I paint along the edge of one pencil line, and then switch hands to do the same thing along the facing pencil line. I hold the brush at about a forty-five degree angle to the line, which is to say I use neither the narrow edge or the width of the brush but something in between.

When finished, these two painting strokes usually have already met in the middle of the line, so there is little filling in to do. However, even though it looks like the surface is covered, my experience tells me that once it dries, I'll see many irregularities. That's my weakness. Judy fired me as a painter more than once.

The paint needs to be distributed evenly by rolling or brushing back and forth a couple of times. You don't want a little bead of paint along the outer edge of the line, as that will soak into the canvas and leave a ragged edge. That means it's good to take an interior stroke first, down the center of the line, to remove any excess from your brush. Then push the brush outward and cover the pencil line.

As I mentioned previously, it's hard to come back and touch up any thin or missed spots, so best to get it right the first time. If you go outside of the line, don't keep trying to even it out, going further and further into the path. I once had someone go a full inch beyond the line trying to even things out. I call this a "boa constrictor" (who just had lunch). If you make a mistake, don't compound it by trying to fix it. Leave it to be dealt with during the detailing. A small mistake is better than turning it into a big mistake.

Put a little piece of colored tape by anything that needs future attention. You might think it will be really obvious, but it will be very hard to find amidst all the lines. You would be surprised how large of an error you can make and still not be noticed by many people. Unless you are me, you don't walk a labyrinth to inspect the workmanship, but to have a personal experience.

A few tricks of the trade

When I became a labyrinth maker, I knew I would either develop a strong back or be crippled for life. Fortunately it has proved to be the former. Nevertheless, we can only take so much crawling around and painting, even if we use dollies. So we developed some alternatives.

One was a painting counter, 13 feet wide, which allowed us to stand while we worked. Each 12' wide section of canvas was rolled up on a long piece of four-inch plastic PVC pipe that sat in a slot at the bottom of the counter.

The canvas was unrolled and pulled up over the counter. As we completed one countertop's worth of lines, we then pulled the canvas forward, exposing a new set of lines to paint. We used clamps to hold the canvas tightly in place. Our room wasn't 36 feet long so we pulled the canvas as far as we could and then stopped for it to dry. In the morning, we rolled up the dry section and repeated the process until the whole piece was completed.

John Bielik using the painting counter which has a bank of lights for better visibility.

61

Some of our patterns comprised a single piece of material, 24' wide. Our painting counter was not that wide. Instead, we lined up four eight-foot tables, end to end, and pulled the canvas across them, just as with the painting counter. Yes, three eight-foot tables would be just wide enough, but using four tables gives space at each end to hold lights, tools, boom box, etc.

Judy painting a 24' Santa Rosa on folding tables.

During labyrinth walks, we like to use a runner at the entrance to the labyrinth, along which we place chairs on each side. People can sit there, remove their shoes, and then walk to the entrance. Labyrinths are often carried in canvas bags. You can paint patterns on the runner or the bags or other items used with the labyrinth to match the color(s) of the labyrinth itself.

If you're painting a Chartres pattern, you might want to use a technique invented by Jim McNamee, a UPS employee who was one of our best part timers at the studio. When taping the concentric circles with the tape machine, he put one extra circle of tape that marked the top of the lunation teeth.

Later, he painted right up onto the tape. Then, when you remove the tape, you will have a perfect top edge and sharp corners. Yes, you can use a tiny brush and try to do 226 corners one at a time, but when you tape the top of the lunation, you can use your regular brush or roller to follow the lunation circle right up onto the tape, with no need to do any corners. No tape machine? You could use the same technique by taping each tooth individually.

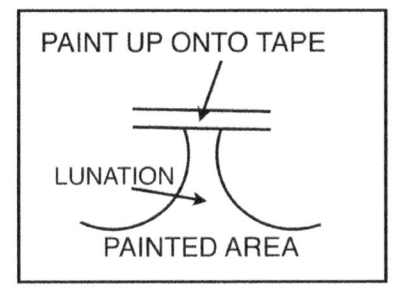

Paint up onto tape. When tape is removed, the corners are finished. No need to use a small brush.

Detailing

If you have some small little drips or bobbles, leave them alone until they dry. Trying to wipe them up will just press paint down into the canvas and make the spot worse. Once dry, scrape them off with the point of a razor knife or compass and use a hard ink eraser on what is left.

For really big mistakes, get some canvas-colored paint and paint over them. It isn't a perfect solution, because matching the color of canvas is next to impossible. That's because the threads in the warp and weft are sometimes different colors. You can only match one of them.

Or just leave your little mistakes. Like beauty marks, they will emphasize the perfection of the rest of the labyrinth. The canvas itself is likely to have some imperfections as well. The value is in the fact that the labyrinth is handmade. It doesn't have to look like it was produced by a machine.

Drawing the perimeter

My first several canvas labyrinths I had the people who did my sewing also cut and hem the perimeter. Then one day, as I was swinging the pencils around for the outer circle, I went right off the canvas. They had gotten the octagon wrong. The problem was they didn't have a space large enough to spread out the whole canvas, so they did it one side at a time. Inaccurately. From that point onward, after the drawing and painting was completed, I drew and cut the perimeter of the canvas myself and then took it back to be hemmed.

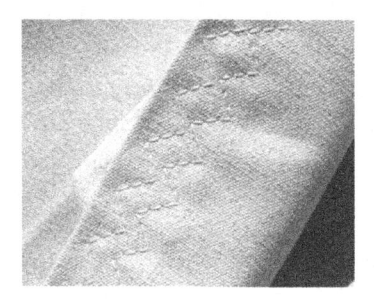

Lars Howlett makes canvas labyrinths and sent me this photo of the neat hemming job by a local company in California.

You can decide what shape you would like the perimeter. Octagonal is very common. One way to draw an octagon is to start with a square and cut off the corners. Measure inward from the corners to the cutoff point. The distance from the corner is equal to 29.29% of the side of the square.

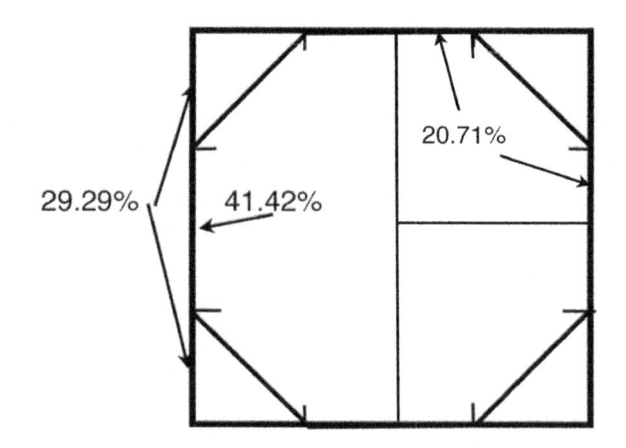

Suppose, for example, that the side of the square (hence, the width of your canvas) is 30'. Since 30' equals 360", multiplying by 29.29% (decimal: .2929) yields 105.44", just a hair over 105 7/16". Measure from the corner down each adjacent side by this distance and then connect the two points. The result should be an equilateral octagon.

If your piece of material is not a square, then you can make an octagon by starting at the center point of each side and measuring that side of the octagon, outward. You already have the horizontal and vertical axes marked. At the edge of the canvas, just measure out from the axis 20.71% of the width of the canvas (which is half of 41.42%, the value for the side of the octagon).

The octagon equals the width of the canvas in both directions, being equilateral. So from the vertical axis, measure out half the canvas width in three places: on the horizontal axis and on the two edges of the canvas. Connect these three points to draw a line that includes the side of the octagon. Then, from the horizontal axis, measure out 20.71% of the canvas width in each direction to find the remaining octagon points.

Before drawing the perimeter lines, measure between the octagon points to see how accurate your measurements are. Make adjustments as needed. I use a straightedge that is two inches wide and draw hem lines on both sides. I trim the canvas on the outer line. The inner one gives a visible indication of where to fold (or double-fold) the canvas for the hem, assuring consistency. A professional doesn't really need such a guide but if you are sewing your own hems it could be helpful.

A Tribute to Judy Hopen

For some fifteen years Judy worked faithfully for Labyrinth Enterprises, LLC. Her name should be remembered as being synonymous with "canvas labyrinths." Actually, she did very well making permanent onsite labyrinths as well, so I'll include a little information about that.

Judy was a client during my brief stint as a massage therapist in St. Louis. In our conversation I found that she was a creative person involved in performance art. She was not happy with her day work because it didn't suit her sensibilities.

Working on the side as a photographer's model, Judy could have had a successful career as a fashion model, had the opportunity presented itself. Her collection of vintage clothing included more than 300 hats and pairs of gloves. At labyrinth gatherings she invariably wore something eye catching, such as a leopard suit and cat eye contact lenses.

Judy had no training or experience in drawing and painting other than sewing and designing costumes. She said she was math phobic and never saw labyrinths in terms of numbers as I do. She saw them as patterns, as an ancient geometer would.

We worked for ten years in the gymnasium of Taproots School of the Arts and five years in our own studio (photo). It was a beautiful workspace, with clerestory windows and plenty of light. It comprised an area of 80' x 100' (8,000 square feet). Part of a historic building (a nineteenth century repair shop for street cars), our studio was restored by the new owner at a cost far exceeding the total of our five years of rent.

To reduce heating bills in the winter, we enclosed 2,800 sq. ft. in a plastic "tent." The labyrinth painted on the floor was an accident, having bled through a thin material we were painting.

Judy's work was mostly behind the scenes, drawing and painting day after day in solitude. She perfected painting while holding a cellphone to her shoulder, racking up thousands of minutes per month. As mistress of the studio she became a patron of the arts holding impromptu concerts and other events.

Judy hated regimented nine-to-five jobs. In the studio, she found her calling. "God, I love this job," she exclaimed often. Due to her chronic fatigue syndrome, she was as likely to be working in the middle of the night as any other time.

Having made or supervised the creation of almost a thousand canvas labyrinths, she must have drawn and painted more labyrinths than anyone in history. We had a few part time workers, but Judy personally did most of the work. Her attention to detail was admirable. We shipped labyrinths to forty-eight states (missing Maine and North Dakota) and fourteen foreign countries.

Once you can draw a labyrinth with a pencil, the next step is to draw it with a saw, scoring the pattern into concrete or pavers.

Judy was excellent with tools and became a supervisor for on-site installations. It was also Judy who organized the rental of canvas labyrinths and filled book orders.

I may be including too much about onsite labyrinths, but this is a favorite photo of Judy on top of two pallets of pavers. She was thin but strong. After this photo was taken, she carried every one of these pavers (almost two tons) into the labyrinth we were making in New Jersey.

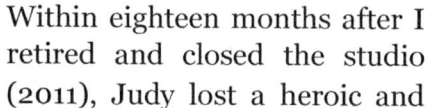

Within eighteen months after I retired and closed the studio (2011), Judy lost a heroic and troubled struggle, dying of breast cancer at the age of 51. Ever a fashionista, she had her bald head tattooed (henna). In her final year she posted this on an internet site:

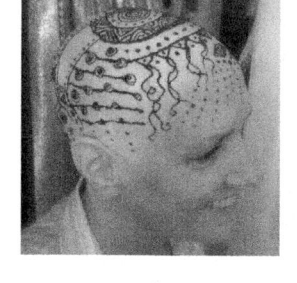

I'm a fellow traveler who is currently in The Great Void, The Great Mystery, due to recent devastation of my world on many levels & in the midst of a life-altering health journey.

She left behind an impressive body of work, a fitting legacy to her outstanding talent. Judy included in her emails a list of her credentials, including studio manager, vice president of Labyrinth Enterprises, LLC, and a title I gave her: *"Labyrintiste extrodinaire."* She was certainly that.

Painting. Note roller and tray setup.

Laying out the measurements and adjusting the masting tape.

Judy drawing petals for a labyrinth in the Bahamas. Note her tool, essentially a yardstick compass but with a Sharpie® marker and a bracket for holding a second. The pens and point are on two separate pieces of yardstick, clamped together (and thus, easily adjustable).

This photo was taken by Lea Goode-Harris. This is how I prefer to remember Judy: happy and relaxed.

Lea Goode-Harris, known for creating the Santa Rosa design, also created a Snoopy labyrinth at the Charles Schultz museum in Santa Rosa. In the photo above, Judy is sitting on the stone that serves as Snoopy's nose!

Snoopy labyrinth (profile). Nose is at far left.

Gallery

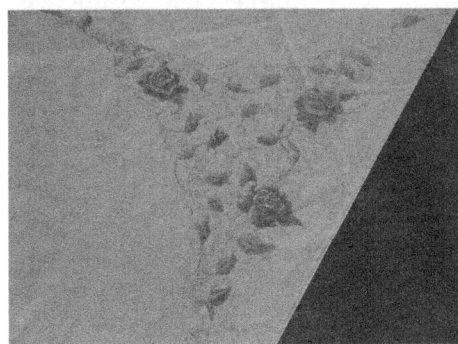

We initiated a series of labyrinths created by guest artists. The first one was noted fabric artist Meryl Ann Butler. Her 12-foot design is filled with light, roses, and even glows in the dark.

Twice we made Santa Rosa labyrinths out of stenciled vines. We made several stencils to avoid looking too repetitive. (As patterns I used leaves from the English ivy in my yard.) Our palette had several colors of green and one of brown.

I used a small bottle with a thin nose to make individual  veins for each leaf, some ten thousand of them total.

After drawing the leaves, we drew the vine that connected them all.

We made two labyrinths like this. While we charged $1,000 extra for the ivy, if I ever do it again, it will be $10,000. (If you're interested, let me know.)

Nefertiti DuBoise on the finished ivy labyrinth. That really is her name. While homeless for a few months she lived in the studio.

A ceremonial labyrinth for weddings (my design). Enter on the sides, get married in the center, leave together out the top. For divorce, reverse the direction.

A Chartres-like 7-circuit design we call the Petite Chartres, 24' in diameter, a single piece (no Velcro®).

In St. Paul, Minnesota, labyrinth designer Lisa Moriarty helped Crossroads Elementary School students and Susan Dustin, the school social worker, to create a canvas labyrinth (see: www.problemsolvinglabyrinth.com) that is used for problem solving and conflict resolution. It's a dual path labyrinth in which two people walk separately and then meet in the middle.

The paths in order: State the Problem, State Your Feelings, State the Other Person's Feelings, Brainstorm Ideas, Choose the Best. In my day, we just duked it out on the playground.

Care Instructions

Canvas needs a certain amount of care. Whether for yourself or to give to a client, it's best to be aware of this information. Note that I don't give warrantees. There is no way of telling how someone will care for a labyrinth. Further, with no moving parts, there is little that can go wrong.

Yes, we have shipped the wrong pattern before, and once or twice, we made a mistake in the design. We shipped a canvas labyrinth all the way to England only to learn that we reversed the turns on a Chartres pattern, putting the left ones on the right side and the right ones on the left side. There were islands which could not be reached.

We devised a plan of how to fix it, by painting over the mistakes and redoing the turns. After replacing the original one for a correct one, we tried to sell the defective one for a big discount. No takers. So we just told them to throw it away. Hopefully someone got a chance to use all of that canvas (on the back) for art work.

Some of the following may be a bit repetitive but I'm including it in one place for your convenience if you wish to share it.

Keep It Clean

It's easier to keep the canvas clean than to try to clean it after it gets dirty. Make sure that people remove their shoes before walking. Socks are preferred to bare feet. If someone needs to wear shoes, they can cover them with the little shoe booties that are available from medical supply stores.

We always place a basket of clean socks near the labyrinth. Walking barefoot can be problematic, as it gets body oils onto the labyrinth. So, we ask people to wear socks. Women wearing nylons may prefer to put on some socks. The socks may also be placed over one's shoes (instead of the booties mentioned above).

Masking tape is another item that can be used to keep the canvas clean. Buy two- or three-inch-wide tape. For wheelchairs, wrap tape around the tire. Tape can also be used on the bottom of walkers. For that matter, people could tape the bottom of their shoes.

Always keep food, drinks, and candles away from the canvas. We once had bottle candles on the floor around the outside of the canvas. In a moment of inattention I kicked one of the bottles which went rolling onto the labyrinth spewing hot red wax everywhere.

You can remove wax by putting something in the freezer, but that's hard with a labyrinth. The iron-and-paper-bag method works to some degree. You can use a razor knife and scape it off. Nothing is ideal.

If you use tape to hold down the canvas, don't use anything that leaves a sticky residue, as this will attract and hold dirt. We recommend gaffer's tape, which is used in theater sets. Or 231, as described earlier.

Before laying out the canvas, clean the floor. Even when clean to the eye, it may be dusty or have some dirt or grease. At the very least use a dust mop and better would be to wash the floor ahead of time. Never use the labyrinth out of doors. It isn't made for that. Even with the best of precautions, there are many things that can happen, and none of them are good.

If you choose to use the labyrinth outdoors despite this recommendation, be sure to put a tarp or plastic under it. Sweep the pavement clean so there are no rocks or sticks that can damage the canvas. Protect it from access by pets or animals or children or people wearing shoes.

When finished, dry it by draping it over chairs or tables, indoors. Make sure it's completely dry before folding, as any moisture can cause mildew. If you do get mildew, don't use liquid cleaners. Vacuum it and use a stiff brush.

Folding the Canvas

When folding the canvas to put it away, the first fold should be in half, so that painted side faces painted side. This protects it from the back of the canvas, which may be dirty. Then, continue to fold it until the proper size for your storage container. When folding, avoid folding directly on the seams. If there is a seam in the middle, fold the labyrinth so that it's a few inches short of being exactly in half, thus avoiding putting a crease on the seam. This protects the paint.

Our large, three-piece labyrinths come with three canvas bags. These are quite large, allowing the labyrinth to be folded into larger sections than when putting them into the plastic bin, thereby reducing the number of creases and wrinkling.

Another possibility is to roll the 12-foot sections onto long pieces of PVC pipe. Of course, this gets the front in contact with the back, so it must be clean on both sides. This is what we do when we are painting the labyrinths on our painting counter. If you have a place to put such pipes, perhaps this might work for you.

It's possible to fold the labyrinth as a single piece rather than undoing the Velcro®. Just roll it into the storage bin (tipped on its side), stand it up, and wheel it away.

Cleaning the labyrinth

Before folding the labyrinth, sweep it with a soft broom. (Keep a new broom to be used only for this purpose, to assure that it's clean.) During the folding process, clean the back of the canvas as it becomes exposed during the folding process.

We've found that we can vacuum the labyrinth. This gets the dirt hiding in the texture of the canvas. Dirt spots can be removed by erasing with a soft eraser. We heard of one group who erased their entire labyrinth, making it look like new again! It must have taken quite a while, and quite a few erasers.

After erasing, use masking tape to pick up the debris from the erasers. Masking tape itself can sometimes be used to remove dirt or lint. We have not found any chemical or liquid that cleans canvas without leaving a ring or other stain. There may be some useful dry powders used for carpet cleaning, but we haven't found them. Any kind of moisture will wrinkle the canvas and cause it to bunch up and shrink.

If there is a very dark stain that can't be removed, you can consider getting some canvas-colored paint and painting over the spot. We have done that in a few rare instances. You can also paint an animal or flower or other figure over that spot.

In the end, if the labyrinth is really dirty, you may wish to take it to a carpet cleaning establishment. We have never tried this, but it might be worthwhile.

Shipping the labyrinth

Always enclose the labyrinth in a plastic container or cardboard carton. While Federal Express will ship the labyrinth in its canvas bags, the bags get filthy.

Be sure to insure the labyrinth for its full value. It costs only a few dollars extra. Don't claim it as artwork, as that can't be insured. It's simply a manufactured labyrinth which happens to be made of canvas.

When shipping to Canada, however, it's possible to avoid paying the high duty charged against textiles by saying that the labyrinth *is* art work, on which there are no duties. After all, it's hand painted on canvas. While avoiding duties, you will not be able to insure the labyrinth for its full value, as there are restrictions for art work.

Labyrinths can also be carried in duffle bags as luggage on an airplane. Customs may have some questions if traveling to a foreign country.

Renting Your Labyrinth

We had eight rental labyrinths which got quite a bit of activity. We charged $150 for two or three days, although I've heard of people charging $200 or more. If the client wanted to keep the labyrinth longer, the price increased. Since we were in the business of selling labyrinths, we always gave the renter the option to buy the used labyrinth at a discount.

We had a number of printed materials and instructions that went with the labyrinth. The renter had to either have insurance or take personal responsibility for the labyrinth. We have had them returned in terrible condition, with grass on them ("No, we didn't use it outdoors.") or candle wax ("We didn't use any candles."). On occasion they were just stuffed into the bin like dirty laundry without even folding them.

For a while we had an outside organization handling our rentals, but their rules were so strict they seemed prohibitive. In any case, certain regulations must be made clear. For example, getting insurance when shipping them back is mandatory.

Once you have a canvas labyrinth, you may be asked by others to use it. Perhaps some of the following forms will be helpful. Your situation won't be the same as ours, so a few of the provisions may not pertain.

Labyrinth Rental Terms and Conditions

By renting a labyrinth from Labyrinth Enterprises, LLC, you agree to abide by these terms and conditions.

PAYMENT DETAILS

Any returned checks shall incur a fee of $35. If rental is cancelled within four weeks of rental date, a fee of $75 shall be retained. The rest of the payment shall be refunded. If the labyrinth is rented by another party for the same dates, only $25 shall be retained to cover office time.

RESPONSIBILITY

The person or organization entering into this agreement ("Renter") hereby takes full responsibility for the care and safekeeping of the labyrinth. If it is damaged, no matter what the cause or circumstances, the renting party shall pay the full cost of repairing or replacing the labyrinth as determined by Labyrinth Enterprises, LLC.

SHIPPING

Renter shall repackage labyrinth according to the instructions and return it the next business day after the rental. In some cases, the labyrinth may be sent directly to the next renter. In such case, Labyrinth Enterprises, LLC, shall provide the name and address for the destination. The labyrinth shall be insured for its full retail value, which will be shown on the rental confirmation form.

LATE RETURN CHARGE

Return to Labyrinth Enterprises, LLC, or the next renter must be done in a timely manner. Each day the renter delays in returning the labyrinth shall be considered another day of rental, at the rate of $50 per day. Failure to return the labyrinth on time could result in another party not having the labyrinth for a scheduled event. In such event, any required expedited shipping shall be paid by Renter.

ACCEPTANCE OF LABYRINTH

The labyrinth may be delivered directly from another renter. If there is any problem, such as the labyrinth being dirty or damaged in shipping or in some way incomplete, please document the situation by taking appropriate photographs and contact Labyrinth Enterprises, LLC, immediately. If we are not contacted until after the rental period, any damage will be the responsibility of the party to this agreement.

CARE AND USE OF LABYRINTH

Renter shall maintain the labyrinth in good repair and operating condition at renter's own cost and effort. The labyrinth may only be used indoors, in a careful and proper manner. The use of the labyrinth must comply with all Terms of Care and Use. If Labyrinth Enterprises, LLC, must expend an inordinate amount of time to restore the labyrinth to rental condition (cleaning, etc.) it shall bill renter accordingly at the rate of $40 per worker hour plus materials and expenses.

ASSIGNMENT

Renter shall not assign this agreement or rent the labyrinth to any other party not specifically included in this agreement unless approved in writing by Labyrinth Enterprises, LLC.

OPTION TO RENEW

If Renter wishes to keep the labyrinth longer and the dates are available, this agreement may be extended. The terms of such extension shall be specified in writing and signed by both parties to this agreement.

OPTION TO PURCHASE

Renter shall have the option to purchase the labyrinth at the end of the lease term for the amount shown on the rental confirmation form. If another rental is pending, the labyrinth may need to be used to fulfill that obligation, after which it will be returned to Renter. Alternatively, 100% of the rental fee may be applied toward any future purchase of a labyrinth from Labyrinth Enterprises, LLC.

LIABILITY AND INDEMNITY

Renter shall indemnify and hold harmless Labyrinth Enterprises, LLC, its officers or employees, from any liability for loss of any kind, injury, disability or death of any person in connection with the use and operation of the labyrinth. Renter should have sufficient liability coverage to protect against any such claims.

ENTIRE AGREEMENT AND MODIFICATION

This agreement constitutes the entire agreement between the parties. No modification or amendment of this agreement shall be effective unless in writing and signed by both parties.

GOVERNING LAW

This Lease shall be construed in accordance with the laws of the State of Missouri.

ARBITRATION

Any controversy or claim relating to this agreement shall be settled by binding arbitration in Saint Louis, Missouri, under the rules of the American Arbitration Association, and any judgment granted by the arbitrator(s) may be enforced in any court of proper jurisdiction.

TERMS OF CARE AND USE

1. The labyrinth must be returned in clean and operable condition. Any necessary cleaning, folding, or other attention shall be billed at the hourly fee stated in the agreement.

2. The labyrinth is designed for indoor use only and is to be laid out on a dry, clean surface devoid of sharp objects which could cause damage.

3. The labyrinth is to be used only with proper foot covering, such as paper booties, clean socks or hose. No uncovered shoes or bare feet are allowed on the labyrinth.

4. The labyrinth must not be secured by any form of adhesive material (e.g., masking or duct tape, glue, etc.). When packing for shipping, do not use duct tape.

5. The labyrinth may not be used in the presence of food, drink, and liquids within the same room.

6. The labyrinth may not be used within 20 feet of a fire source or open flame (e.g., candles, smudge sticks, etc.). This includes enclosed flames, such as bottle candles. Use of battery-operated votive or bottle candles is acceptable.

7. The labyrinth must be returned in its storage container. If not, Renter shall be charged for a new shipping container.

If you wish to include for your event an informative display regarding the history and use of labyrinths, download the free poster set from www.labyrinth-enterprises.com/posters.html.

We provide labyrinth rentals as a public service. Thank you for your cooperation in following the above instructions. Please contact us if you have any suggestions for our rental procedures.

Confirmation by renter:

I have read and agree to the above terms and conditions, and terms of care and use.

Printed
Name_____

Signature_____

Labyrinth pattern_____

Rental dates_____

Date of this agreement_____

LABYRINTH RENTAL

Before executing this agreement, check with Labyrinth Enterprises, LLC, Studio Division, to make sure the desired dates are available. Email Judy Hopen or call (314) 865-1988 or (314) 922-5839. Paste this document into an email and fill it out, or fax it and send it to (314) 865-1988 (call first so we can turn on the fax).

LABYRINTH RENTED:

_____Chartres(36')

_____Santa Rosa (24')

_____Petite Chartres (24')

_____Small Classical (18')

_____Large Classical (24')

_____Twin Hearts (22' x 28')

DATES OF EVENT:

From _____

To _____

RENTER:

Contact Name_____

Organization_____

Address_____

City_____ State_____ Zip_____

Telephone number(s)_____

Email_____

Website_____

COST:

Rental fee _____

Shipping _____

Total_____

PAYMENT:

_____Check mailed (remit to studio address below)

_____Mastercard or Visa

Card number_____

Exp_____

Billing address for credit card (if different)

_____

_____

Shipping address (if different)

_____

_____

PLEASE REMIT PAYMENT AND HARD COPY TO:

Labyrinth Enterprises, LLC, Studio
2725 S. Jefferson Avenue
Saint Louis, MO 63118-1506

By renting this labyrinth and signing below (physically or electronically), renter acknowledges having read the Terms and Conditions, and the Terms of Care and Use. The terms include important details regarding financial responsibilities and duties of the renter who signs below.

I, _____, agree to the Terms and Conditions and the Terms of Care and Use for this labyrinth.

Printed name_____

Date_____

Addendum

When making, labyrinths, renting them, or using them, we often have an opportunity to share with people information about the history and use of labyrinths. When I first began working with labyrinths, they were virtually unknown. Now, everywhere I go people seem to be familiar with them.

So, maybe it isn't as important now to spread the word. Nevertheless, I've included below typical flyers that we make available during labyrinth walks and presentations.

About Labyrinths

A labyrinth is a pattern, generally two-dimensional, in which a series of lines delineate a pathway which is meant to be walked. Labyrinths are ancient, going back to pre-history. Being mostly circular, labyrinths reflect the basic movement of creation, identified in the spherical shape and movement of planets and atoms alike. The movement of the zodiac, the seasons, phases of the moon, tides, life and death—nature is cyclical. Labyrinths serve as a microcosm of the universe we inhabit.

It is very important to distinguish between a labyrinth and a maze. *Labyrinth* is used to identify a pattern that has a single path which, although it may be circuitous, leads unfailingly to the center without any intersections or choices to make. *Maze,* on the other hand, connotes a complex pattern with many paths, intersections, choices, dead ends, and false passages.

What also distinguishes mazes and labyrinths is the completely opposite mental states they elicit. A maze involves a contest, a puzzle to be solved. It requires constant mental and intellectual effort. It involves a competition between the walker and the maze designer. A labyrinth, on the other hand, requires no such effort. The mind can completely relax, but because the path is circuitous, one must still pay attention. That state of awareness, combined with a relaxed mind, is typical of meditation. For that reason, the labyrinth is frequently seen as a means of walking meditation.

What happens when walking a labyrinth varies from person to person. Most commonly, people report a sense of peace, relaxation, and well-being. Some have reported emotional healing, such as dealing with grief or contemplating one's next step in life. Labyrinths are thought to restore a sense of equilibrium and balance, which can be especially helpful when our lives seem overburdened or out of kilter.

Many people are surprised by the rapport they feel with labyrinths. Often they are unable to verbalize it, only to feel it. The labyrinth takes us out of our modern rectilinear perspective. It rescues us from the busyness and pressure of schedules and responsibilities and gives us time to be with ourselves in a focused way. We may find comfort or relaxation, or encounter our deeper and more authentic selves. Perhaps we tap into a long-forgotten archetypal reservoir that reconnects us with the universe, our ancient predecessors, and ourselves.

With the mind and emotions calmed and the body in a greater state of balance and equilibrium, we have the opportunity to go below the surface of things. The intellect can take a break. We can go deep within, to our authentic selves. In a heightened state of awareness, insights sometimes occur when walking the labyrinth, drawing on a far greater wisdom and vision than is normally accessible.

Getting past the rational mind is the goal of most spiritual paths, using methods such as prayer, surrender, and meditation. The Rev. Dr. Lauren Artress has written, "Most of the experiences that occur in the labyrinth are unexpected. They are guided by a sacred wisdom, a creative intelligence that knows more about what we need than do our conscious selves."

The labyrinth lends itself to expressing our intent and making our supplications. Stating our intent and then walking the labyrinth makes the purpose clear to ourselves and to higher powers. There is no particular experience that is supposed to happen when walking the labyrinth. The effects of the labyrinth are cumulative. The more you walk, the greater will be the benefits.

Labyrinth Instructions

Some reasons to walk the labyrinth
    To pray
    To meditate
    To relax
    To feel inner peace
    To gain equilibrium, balance
    To express intent
    To ask a question
    For inspiration
    To gain clarity
    To be in the present moment
    For physical healing
    For emotional healing
    To assuage grief
    As a pilgrimage
    As a spiritual practice
    For spiritual growth
    To enhance inspiration, creativity

For ceremony or ritual
For personal time out
To be refreshed
Just for fun

Preparation for Walking
Wait until there is enough room for you in the labyrinth.
Please remove your shoes or cover them with something.
Please do not talk or disrupt the peaceful ambiance.
Remember that you are participating in an ancient spiritual practice.
Breathe deeply, center yourself, and put other things out of mind.
If you wish, invoke the presence of a higher force for guidance.
Pause at the entrance to bow or in some way acknowledge the labyrinth.

Walking the Labyrinth
Walk at your own pace.
There may be two-way traffic. Cooperate with others.
It is OK to pass others, or to be passed. This is done best at the turns.
Be aware of your experience, your body, your thoughts and feelings.
Pause in the center if you wish to meditate there.
Return by the same path you entered or, if you choose, walk directly out.
Upon exiting, turn and again acknowledge the labyrinth.

After Leaving the Labyrinth
Continue to be aware of your labyrinth experience.
Take a moment to sit quietly and reflect on your walk.
You may wish to journal or draw to express your experience.
Thank yourself for the gift you have given yourself.
Walk the labyrinth again, as many times as you wish.
Tell friends of your experience and invite them to come walk.

Drawing Instructions

This book is meant to give all necessary information for the average person to work with canvas as a medium. It's not meant to be a manual on how to make labyrinths in general. We have two other books on that topic, one for the Chartres pattern and one for the classical labyrinth. However, it would seem to be incomplete to not at least give a few basic pointers.

Drawing the Chartres Pattern

Although it looks complicated, the Chartres pattern can be accomplished one step at a time, drawing in the following order:

1. Laying out the axes, circle spacing, and back-to-back turns (called labryses).

2. Drawing the entrance lines.

3. Making the circles

4. Adding the turns

5. Adding the petals in the center

6. Finishing up with the lunations around the perimeter

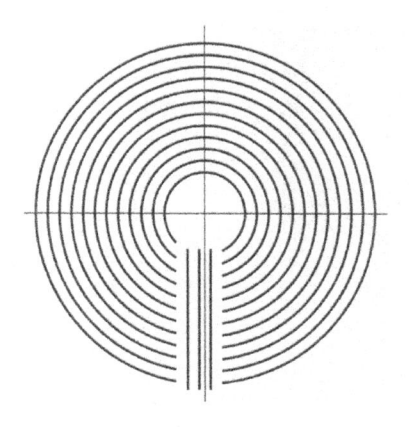

Notice that the central entrance path (that will lead into the center) is centered on the vertical axis. The entrance into the labyrinth is in the lower left quadrant.

By drawing the entrance paths first, you avoid making circles in pathways, which would require extensive erasing.

This drawing (above) was made for making masking tape labyrinths, in which you make all of the circles and then remove some tape for the turns. You won't want to do that in pencil, as it would require too much erasing. Instead, mark out the start and stop points for each circle prior to drawing it (and for the entrance lines as well). Be sure to mark the starting point at the entrance, the stopping point for the turn (each circle has one), where to start up again, and where to stop at the entrance.

You can prepare for making your canvas labyrinth by making some small practice drawings on paper. By studying the pattern, you will become familiar with the location of the various elements. For this purpose I include a full drawing.

Notice, for example, that the turns at the entrance are in pairs. The left side and the right side are the same, turned 180-degrees to each other. At the top, the turns are at circles 2, 5, 8, and 11. On the right side they are 3, 6, and 9. On the left they are 4, 7, and 10.

I've made so many labyrinths that these numbers are ingrained in my mind. Often I don't even refer to a drawing when making a labyrinth.

Note that you will be drawing two lines for each circle, and painting between them. I number from the inside outward, circle 1-i (inner), 1-o (outer), 2-i, 2-o, and so forth. You don't really need to draw 1-i because it will be the petals, or 12-o, as it will become the lunations. Here is the pattern again, with double lines.

In the center, there are six petals. When two petal circles meet and form the petal cross, the lines overlap, so there is only one line width. It's this overlapping that pushes the circles aside enough to allow for the entrance.

The outer petal circles are one-third the diameter of the center. The tips of the petal crosses are at the mid-radius point (from 1-0). These relationships are shown in the following drawing.

The relationship between the petals and the center circle.

There is a very popular variation of the Chartres pattern, originated by Veriditas. In it, the turns have more space between them (easier to see, a place to step off the path) and the space between the petals are filled in.

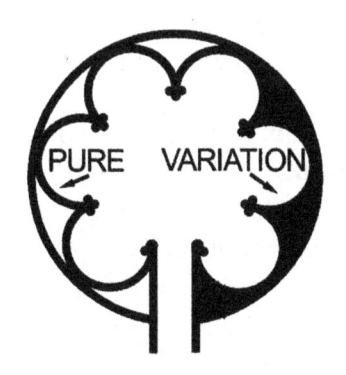

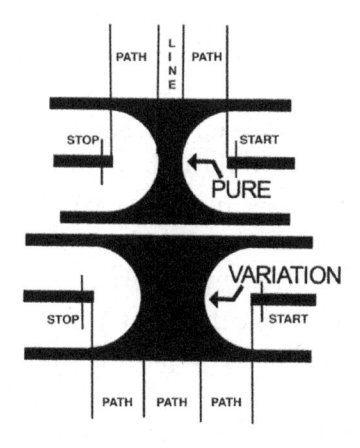

If you make the variation, make the entrance turns half a path width.

Proportions of the labyrinth

All of the elements of the labyrinth relate to each other, as described below.

Center diameter: One-fourth the diameter of the labyrinth, as measured from the outside of the first and twelfth circles (not counting the lunations).

Petal diameter (outside line): One-third the diameter of the center circle.

Path width: One-third the outer diameter of the petal.

Lunation spacing: The same as the path width.

Line width: Divide the width of the path by 4.5, or, divide the path by 9 and multiply that result by two.

Petal crosses: The tips of the crosses at the ends of the petals are exactly one-half the distance from the center of the labyrinth to the outer first circle. In other words, they are located at one-half the length of the 1-o (circle one, outer) radius.

Lunation circle: The partial circle of the lunation and the width of the adjacent teeth have a proportion, not surprisingly, of 9:2, just like the paths and lines. Just as the path was 9/11 of the whole path/line unit, so the lunation circle is 9/11 of the lunation unit (circle plus tooth width), which is equal to the path width. That's a bit complicated to understand at first reading. The path is 9/11 of the path/line unit, and then it becomes the whole unit for lunation spacing, of which the lunation circle is 9/11 of that.

Tooth height: The teeth between the lunation circles are roughly the same height (from the inside of the 12th circle to the tip of the tooth) as the diameter of the lunation circle. This achieves an eye-pleasing 1:1 ratio between the height of the teeth and the space between them.

Labrys width: The bow-tie-shaped figures formed by the back-to-back, 180-degree turns on the labyrinth are separated by a distance slightly wider than the width of the line (at Chartres, 3 1/4" vs. the line of 3").

Here are typical examples of Chartres labyrinth proportions.

Size	12th Circle (outer)	1st Circle (outer)	Petal (outer)	Path & Lunation	Line Width
100'	97' 1"	24' 3"	8' 1"	2' 8 3/8"	7 3/16"
50'	48' 6 1/2"	12' 1 11/16"	4' 9/16"	1' 4 1/16"	3 5/8"
42' 3 3/8"	41' 1/2"	10' 3 1/8"	3' 5 1/16"	1' 1 11/16"	3"
40'	38' 10"	9' 8 1/2"	3' 2 7/8"	1' 1"	2 7/8"
35'	33' 11 3/4"	8' 5 15/16"	2' 10"	11 5/16"	2 1/2"
30'	29' 1 1/2"	7' 3 3/8"	2' 5 3/15"	9 3/4"	2 3/16"

Making lunations strikes terror in the hearts of first timers. A number of sources say that there are 28½ lunations in each quadrant, but that is incorrect. In fact, none of the quadrants have that number. Because the entrance path is to the left of center, that side of the labyrinth has fewer lunations (55 teeth, 55 ½ circles).

There is a tooth at the top, on the vertical axis, and then 57 teeth on the right side (with 57 ½ circles). There would have been 114 of everything, but one lunation is missing for the entrance. So there are 113. For the lunation circles, there are 112 complete ones, plus one-half on either side of the entrance.

The number 112 is 4 x 28, with 28 being a lunar number representing the Virgin Mary. They also used the lunar calendar for determining the date for Easter.

The spacing for the lunations is very close to the width of the line if everything is drawn in the proper proportion. To use the template I've designed and described, mark out where the circle hits the 12th circle, rather than the teeth. Start at the entrance and work toward the top. Adjust your spacing until it comes out right.

Voila, a Chartres labyrinth. That wasn't so hard. You'll find many contemporary 7-circuit Chartres-like designs. Here is the one that I like the best, which I call the Chartres Essence. The center is made larger than normal (one-third the diameter rather than one-fourth) to hold more people.

The Chartres Essence design.

How to Draw a Classical Labyrinth

Looking at the classical labyrinth we notice several things. First, it isn't symmetrical. That's because the vertical arm of the cross connects to the end of one of the top half-circles. If it connects on the left side of the circle, as above, the first turn will be to the left and it will be called a left handed labyrinth. If the opposite were true, it would be right handed.

Note that the turns are symmetrical in relation to each other. Finally, note that the mushroom shape indicates the classical labyrinth must have more than one center for the arcs. In fact, there are five.

This pattern is one of the most popular and ancient designs. It can be drawn by first making what is known as the seed pattern and then connecting the elements. That's not how you will want to draw it on canvas, but the seed pattern is instructional in showing where the centers are.

The dots in the seed pattern represent the ends of the lines. The top of the pattern is made of half-circles, the center for which is obvious. The remaining four centers are at the ends of the lines.

This illustration shows the five center points for the arcs that make the classical labyrinth.

I've described how to use the center post, weights, and tape measure compass. When making the classical labyrinth, you must move the center post to each of the five places (although for the lower quadrants, I often just use a yardstick compass).

Note that the center of the labyrinth is not the center of the top circles. It's one path width higher than that. This is important to know if you are trying to fit the pattern fully onto a piece of canvas.

For most uses, the center of the classical labyrinth is very limiting. It's really just the end of the path. I always make the center larger. When you do that, it has certain repercussions on the geometry. For whatever distance you expand the center, the lower right quadrant moves outward by the same amount since it emanates from the upper right line end, which moves outward as the center gets bigger.

In turn, that moves the lower right quadrant away from the entrance. The phenomenon is shown in the drawing to the left.

We must connect the quadrant with the entrance by using straight lines.

This is a very inefficient way to make a large center. If you really need a traditional classical labyrinth, then go ahead. Otherwise, I'd chose a circular pattern, as the center is larger. You can make the classical pattern round, or use any number of other circular labyrinth designs. I will give a few quick suggestions in the following pages.

Meanwhile, here are the steps for drawing a classical labyrinth with expanded center.

The larger the center, the more flattened the labyrinth becomes.

When the classical is drawn as a circular pattern, the entrance into the center is pushed off to the right. This can be remedied by moving everything over to the left. In the process of doing that, another geometry appears, namely, lining up the two entrance paths on the vertical axis. In such case, there is a small space in the fourth circle that is not used, often called the altar space.

It's just one more step to go from this arrangement to adding internal turns. In doing so, we have changed the classical pattern to such an extent that it begins to resemble a medieval labyrinth.

When I do my labyrinth making master classes, I make a big deal out of that derivation.

Left is a contemporary design known as the Santa Rosa pattern, originated by Lea Goode-Harris who, not surprisingly, lives in Santa Rosa, California. This pattern is copyrighted. Permission to make it is freely given except in commercial situations. Contact Lea at: www.labyrinthtales.com.

Here is another pattern with aligned entrance paths, called the Circle of Peace, originated by Lisa Moriarty in Minnesota. Her website is www.canvaslabyrinths.com.

One good thing about contemporary designs such as the Santa Rosa and the Circle of Peace is that they come with no associations, religious, secular, pagan, or otherwise.

Business Advice

In 2002 I gave a keynote address at the annual meeting of the Labyrinth Society, held that year in Sacramento, California. In it, I shared my business philosophy. The comments below are from that talk.

When we talk about a labyrinth business, we come to a contradiction. Business and labyrinths are two different worlds. Churches have the same problem. Sometimes the religion business gets in the way of finding God. A labyrinth business. Hm-m-m-m-m. I have dealt with this oxymoron for quite some time. As a result, I have developed a number of principles that I think pertain.

1) If we are going to get labyrinths into the world, it must become a viable business. This is a commercial society. We must talk their language. That was a big point in Lauren Artress's talk at the Denver gathering: Know your audience, and speak their language. I once asked Pat Rodegast, during a session in which she was channeling the entity Emmanuel, whether it's good to become a master of illusion, of living within the illusion. Emmanuel said, "Yes, as long as you don't believe it."

2) Secondly, we must charge enough for our services to generate enough income to live on. To some, this seems sacrilegious; it seems like the commercialization of the labyrinth. People have heated debates about copyrighting labyrinth designs, or registering trademarks. Promoting labyrinths takes resources, and business creates such resources. Institutions and architects, for example, are used to paying a rate consistent with professionalism.

3) We must maintain our personal values. Going into business doesn't mean destroying the ecology, cutting down rainforests, or doing unethical things. My particular style is to be low-tech. I know that the sign industry has the technology for making labyrinths with computers and stencils. I prefer the human touch of drawing and painting by hand. The irregularity is pleasing to the eye, and it has a favorable energy component.

4) I've never considered drawing labyrinths to be proprietary information. Perhaps that is true for certain artistic techniques, but not the knowledge essential to making labyrinths. We have always supplied that information to everyone. The same is true with competition. I prefer to see it as collaboration. We are have the same goal: To get labyrinths out into the world.

5) And last, I think it's important to give something back. If you have benefitted from labyrinths, either financially or in some other way, I think it's important to give something back. In my case, it took the form of planning four labyrinth conferences, two in St. Louis in 1997 and 1998, at which the Labyrinth Society was formed, and then the first two gatherings, in Denver (1999) and Fayetteville (2000). When I discovered that the world's greatest labyrinth compendium existed only in German, I wrote to the publisher and began the process that led to the new English edition. Jeff Saward and I worked for three years editing this volume, for which we receive no royalties or compensation. All payment goes to Mrs. Kern, who is still alive and who, quite frankly, needs it.

Resources

There are two nonprofit organizations that every labyrinth person should know about.

<u>Veriditas</u>   www.veriditas.org

Founded in 1995 as Veriditas, the World Wide Labyrinth Project, this organization continues to be the leading source of events and training of facilitators. It's for them that I do a master class each summer. The proceeds from my labyrinth books go to Veriditas.

<u>The Labyrinth Society</u>   www.labyrinthsociety.org

I organized the meetings in St. Louis, Missouri, in 1997 and 1998 that led to the formation of The Labyrinth Society. It has grown to be a very influential and supportive force in promoting labyrinths, from the annual gatherings to the creation of an excellent video to a well-designed website. If you are interested in labyrinths, you should be a part of this organization.

<u>Labyrinth Locator</u>   www.labyrinthlocator.com

Co-founded by the above two organizations, this website lists labyrinths around the world. If you own a labyrinth or build one for others, be sure to have it listed here.

<u>Labyrinth Enterprises, LLC</u>   www.labyrinth-enterprises.com

This is my company's website and the publisher of my books. We are still fully in the business of designing, consulting, and building labyrinths, even though I personally only work on the occasional project. We were founded in 1995, the first full-time full-service labyrinth company.

Labyrinthos   www.labyrinthos.net

This is the website for Jeff Saward, the world's leading authority on labyrinths. It's a wealth of information. Jeff has the largest collection of labyrinth photos in existence, often supplying material for books and articles. He and his wife Kimberly lead tours of labyrinths and megalithic sites in Great Britain. They met at the meeting in St. Louis in which the Labyrinth Society was formed.

Santa Rosa Labyrinth   www.srlabyrinthfoundation.com

I've mentioned the Santa Rosa labyrinth several times in these pages. Here is a website by its originator, Lea Goode-Harris, about this contemporary design. Lea is available for consultation and custom labyrinths.

Circle of Peace   www.pathsofpeace.com

Circle of Peace, design by Lisa Gidlow Moriarty. She also sells wooden finger labyrinths. Since closing our studio, I've directed clients looking to purchase canvas labyrinths to three sources. Lisa is one. The other two are listed below.

Lars Howlett   www.discoverlabyrinths.com

For several years Lars served as my apprentice and is now a labyrinth maker in his own right, including canvas, temporary, art installations, and permanent onsite. He represents the next generation of labyrinth builders of which I am sure he will be a leading light. Lars has the exclusive license to sell canvas Santa Rosa labyrinths. He is also a professional photographer.

John Ridder   www.paxworks.com

John made his first labyrinth in February, 1995, predating mine. He also sells finger labyrinths and other products.

Postscript

This is the beginning not the end.

Now that you have the capability to make canvas labyrinths, many possibilities present themselves. As you build labyrinths, I hope you will become involved in the labyrinth community.

I also very much value your comments and insights into this book. It's the first edition, which will change and be upgraded regularly. You can assist in this process by any corrections, additions, changes or suggestions that you make.

Janice Hollinger did just that, sending more than a dozen corrections (shame on me). Many thanks. Are there any more?

Once you begin to make labyrinths, be sure to send me a note, and include a photo. Many thanks.

Robert Ferré
robert@labyrinth-enterprises.com

Photo Credits

Most of the photos used in this book were my own, with the follow exceptions, for which I'm grateful.

Page 3   Ruth Hanna
Page 8   Top: Linda Ricketts
Page 11   Unknown, collection of Robert Ferré
Page 14   Warren Lynn
Page 15   Lars Howlett (www.discoverlabyrinths.com)
Page 18   Ruth Hanna
Page 21   Internet, website no longer current
Page 22   Internet, multiple websites, source unknown
Page 41   Top: Internet (credited, http://store.sealcoating.com)
            Bottom: Unknown, collection of Robert Ferré
Page 44   Internet (credited, www.dickblick.com)
Page 48   Unknown, collection of Lars howlett
Page 50   Internet (credited, www.racatac.com)
Page 64   Lars Howlett (www.discoverlabyrinths.com)
Page 67   Unknown, from collection of Judy Hopen
Page 69   Top: Unknown, collection of Judy Hopen
Page 70   Center: Unknown (Internet page of Judy Hopen)
Page 71   Middle: Unknown, collection of Robert Ferré
            Bottom: Unknown, collection of Judy Hopen
Page 72   Top: Lea Goode-Harris (www.labyrinthtales.com)
            Bottom: Internet, Charles Schultz Museum
Page 74   Right: Judy Hopen
Page 76   Lisa Gidlow Moriarty
Page 95   Ruth Hanna

Notes and drawings

Notes and drawings

Made in the USA
Las Vegas, NV
20 December 2021